Periodisation of History:
Arunachal Pradesh

Periodisation of History: Arunachal Pradesh

Prasanta Kumar Nayak

KALPAZ

ISBN: 978-93-5128-219-8

Price: ₹ 680

First Published, 2017

Published by

Kalpaz Publications
C-30, Satyawati Nagar,
Delhi – 110052
E-mail: kalpaz@hotmail.com
Ph.: 9212142040

Printed at: G. Print Process, Delhi

Cataloging in Publication Data—DK

Courtesy: D.K. Agencies (P) Ltd. <docinfo@dkagencies.com>

Nayak, P. K. (Prasant Kumar), 1967- **author.**

Periodisation of history : Arunachal Pradesh / Prasanta Kumar Nayak.

pages cm

Includes bibliographical references.

ISBN 9789351282198

1. Arunāchal Pradesh (India)—History—Periodization. I. Title.

DS485.N68N39 2016 DDC 954.163 23

Contents

Preface

History of a particular people is not overnight made. It is a process in continuity. It is the origin and clan structure of the people, their socio- politico- religious- cultural ethos which largely determine the course of history to be written on them. Documentation of all such ethos is an important tool of history. More is the documentation; merrier is the richness of history. People's contact and exposure with the outside world happens to be dynamic nomenclature to see history growing and gaining momentum. Human history is replete with all such examples. Civilisational habitations, structures, tools used, goods exchanged or traded, engineering and architectural skills, acumen, entrepreneurship and their subsequent applications leave sufficient cornerstones at respective fields for history to shape leaving bias and prejudices apart.

Periodisation in history has been the attempt to categorise or divide historical time into discrete named blocks. It is a complex problem in history. History is in fact continuous and so all systems of periodisation are to some extent arbitrary. Almost every dynamic age is an "age of transition" as the cliche has it. It is nevertheless necessary to divide up history in order to make sense of the past and to articulate changes over time. However, for the sake of convenience, periodisation has been taken as necessary and the historians have broadly divided the entire range of Indian history into three periods i.e., Hindu, Muslim and British or the more appropriate divisions like Ancient, Medieval and Modern. But there is no consensus among the historians to fix the border line between these periods. There will indeed be some uncertainty over where the ancient period ends and the medieval begins, but the triadic division is retained with a difference of a few centuries by one and all.

The history of Arunachal Pradesh has been constructed largely from oral sources passed down from generation to generation, in verse and song. The Ahom *Buranjis* (chronicles of the Ahom kings of Assam) and some archaeological finds that have been unearthed in the area have helped to reconstruct the history. While the land has been inhabited since pre- historic times, it has not come under the direct rule of the British or indeed under the rule of any king in Delhi. The Ahoms did not rule over the hills of present-day Arunachal Pradesh, but they did maintain contact with the people who lived there. Their primary motivation was to protect their empire from depredation by hill tribes and to exercise control over the trade between the regions. Few trade routes passed through the hill tracts to Tibet and on to China. Occasionally, they undertook a 'show of force' exercise, much as the British did, hundreds of years later.

Scant written record available has impeded greatly the study of the history of Arunachal Pradesh. Absence of a script among the tribes inhabiting the region has been a major drawback for documenting aspects of tribal life for their presentation before the readers in black and white as contours of history. The history of the region, hence, becomes all the more patchy and fragmented. But the written record has not been the only source of seeking information about the progress and development of the mankind- the subject matter of history. No doubt, there are certain handicaps in reconstructing the history of Arunachal Pradesh; yet there are certain justifiable sources that help us to a considerable extent to draw an account of the area.

There has been the problem of putting the history of Arunachal into those parameters which have brought in the divisions of Indian history. Asking regional history to pass through the rigors of three-band periodisation keeping its basics insular has invited fallacies in history to grow. Even if we accept in a broader framework the terminating dates for the division of the Ancient, Medieval and Modern periods of Indian history, it cannot be applied fully to the regional history, specifically to the history of Deccan and South India, Eastern, north-eastern and frontier India. Whatever way the periodisation in Indian history has been made, it is mainly based on the history of the Northern India with its geographical thrust on the Ganges valley. Looking at the structure of history of the whole of India such division is not acceptable, because there is no uniform and common date for the establishment of Muslim rule in India. The arrival of Muslims in different parts varies from time to time which raises question of validity of transition of regional history from Ancient to Medieval. Similarly, the foundation of British rule which is taken as the beginning of the Modern period varies at different regions of India asking the historians to believe in a different period of beginning of the Modern history.

History of Arunachal Pradesh experiences too certain trajectories to construe to the above discussed three-fold divisions. The present investigation has been an attempt to carry out research on how best the regional history with reference to the history of Arunachal Pradesh stands justified to such historical narratives so as to come dittoing the periodisation- dictum of Indian history and if found apart, what problems it has really thrown on the scholars. This is what the subject matter has been emphasised upon. The attempt focuses on a sketchy description of the history of the state-history of the origin of the inhabitant-tribes; trends of socialisation; history peeping through social and political trends; British colonial interests over the areas; sources speaking history; periodisation vs. history of Arunachal Pradesh, citing certain ancient, medieval and modern conjectures whether justifiably being put into the parameters of periodisation-issue of Indian history or not and if not problems thereby if any.

I am indebted to the **Indian Council of Historical Research, New Delhi** for funding me this Research Project on '**History of Arunachal Pradesh: A Probe into its**

Periodisation' without which the work on the topic would have been a remote possibility.

The study has stood basically on primary and secondary sources, i.e., the government reports, published books, monographs, research journals and proceedings volumes of Indian History Congress and North East India History Association etc. It has been made possible due to my visit to different Libraries, Archives, Museums and Research Institutes for collection of data. Briefly to name them are Arunachal Pradesh State Library and Museum, Itanagar and Main Library, Rajiv Gandhi University, Itanagar; Assam State Library, Guwahati, Main Library, Gauhati University, Guwahati, National Library, Kolkata and National Archives, New Delhi. Attending the 30th Session of North East India History Association held at Khagarijan College, Nagaon, Assam from 5-7th November 2009 and 71st Session of Indian History Congress held at Gaur Banga University, Malda, West Bengal from 11-13th February, 2010 along with research papers and getting relevant feedback from the historian-participants related to this project on my interactions with them have helped me substantially to reach out to the target.

My sincere gratitude is due to Dr Hage Lasa, Principal, Government College, Yachuli, Arunachal Pradesh (Formerly Principal, Government College, Bomdila, Arunachal Pradesh) who provided me the constant source of inspiration all through the days for the successful completion of the work. I am highly obliged to Professor B. K. Tripathy, Department of History, Indira Gandhi National Tribal University, Amarkantak, Madhya Pradesh (Formerly Professor, Department of History, Rajiv Gandhi University, Itanagar, Arunachal Pradesh) and Professor A. K. Thakur, Department of History, North-Eastern Hill University, Shillong, Meghalaya for their valuable suggestions at various stages of the study. Dr Tasi Taloh, Principal, I. G. G. College, Tezu, Arunachal Pradesh and Dr J. K. Pattnaik, Associate Professor in the Department of Political Science of my college have been in many ways helpful sharing their views with me related to this work. I express my heartfelt thanks to them. I am equally obliged to a number of other persons for rendering me either direct or indirect help and co-operation whenever needed to see this work complete.

My family members also take away the best of my success. Their often unobtrusive, discreet but effulgent kind of intervention and warn on this work asking me to march ahead remain close to my heart. Wife's serious illness during the project period which at one time pushed me to a dark veil of despair never could deter me from visiting several research institutes for collection of data with regard to my work. She has been an 'inspiration' on to the track.

This work is expected to throw new light on periodisation-issue of the history of Arunachal Pradesh and ask readers to benefit.

Tezu
Date: 03.04. 2016

Dr Prasanta Kumar Nayak
Associate Professor
Department Of History
Indira Gandhi Government College
TEZU
Arunachal Pradesh- 792 001

Chapter - 1

Introduction

Arunachal Pradesh once called "terra incognita"[1] and formerly called NEFA, is the north eastern most state of the Indian Union. Covering a geographical area of 83,743 sq. kilometres and accounting for about 2.55 per cent of the total area of the country, it emerged as a full- fledged state in 1987 after a long period of probation under the Nehruvian model of tribal development, enshrined in the *Panchsheel* of tribal policy. In fact, the evolution and formation of Arunachal Pradesh is a tribute to this farsighted tribal policy enunciated by Dr Verrier Elwin in its early stages. The Arunachalees joined the mainstream of Indian political system on their terms after ensuring the insularity of their cultural heterogeneity.

The entire state is almost a rugged mountainous terrain with beautiful green valleys drained by innumerable rivulets and mighty rivers cascading down from the upper elevations. Geologically, the area consists mainly of shale, schist and conglomerates of the Himalayan system. It roughly lies between the latitudes 26^{0}30'N and longitudes 91^{0}30'E and 97^{0}30'E. Geographically, forming India's International Frontier with China and Tibet along the snow- clad mountains in the extreme north, the territory of Arunachal extends from its meeting point with Bhutan to the western direction for approximately 1,030 kilometres in an eastern direction and then taking a turn to the south-east, it forms India's border with Myanmar for about 441 kilometres, following the crest of the Patkai ranges of mountains. At the end of the line in the extreme east, the borders of India, China and Myanmar meet to form the famous tri-junction.

Communicational remoteness and geographical comeuppance rendered the state largely isolated from the rest of the country and impeded progress of historical and scientific investigation. Still the area never did remain completely cleft from the mainstream politics, history, culture and development. This could be made possible due to the strenuous efforts of the officials and administrators and occasional explorations by scientists and surveyors. Historically, Arunachal Pradesh became the cynosure of the British administration when China started throwing her predominance over Tibet (contiguous to Arunachal in its north-west) at the beginning of the twentieth century which landed up in the occupation of Lhasa in 1910. Since then extensive survey operations came off in the area to put more details of the territory and its inhabitants on record. Finally, the independence of the country brought in its train the greater attention and responsibility of the Indian Union to address its developmental issues left uncared so far, given the sensibility of the area remaining close to China in its boundary under the Nehruvian model of tribal policy.

Since Arunachal Pradesh is located well inside the Himalayan mountain ramparts, it provides a safety valve against the invasion from China and Myanmar. It is because of this fact that Arunachal has always caused the curiosity in historians, scholars, politicians and rulers whether being the British or the Indians. Before the arrival of the British in this region, the Ahom rulers of Assam had left no stone unturned to establish their suzerainty over the hill people living in the frontier areas. Somewhat they had succeeded also. The British rulers too, when came in contact with these people applied their best efforts to win over the tribal people of the North East Frontier and subjugated their lands to the British India. Strategic importance of the areas was but the greatest concern for them. To achieve the end the twin principles of conciliation and subjugation were the justified means. The history of Assam bears testimony to the fact that the rulers of Myanmar, even during the British period, made several invasions over the hill territories of Assam to annex them to Myanmar.

In nineteenth century, as also in the early twentieth a thorough study of the culture of the Indian people was undertaken by nationalist scholars and the past was glorified. But the frontiers still remained insular.[2] The political parties and their activities hardly had the scope to be a part of the nationalistic and patriotic upsurge. It remained out of the stream of India's national development. That does not mean that no account of this secluded land was available. Right from the beginning of the British rule in India, it had caught the attention of the British and reports on its people were prepared even before the annexation of Assam to the Company's territories.

To reach out to the inaccessible hilly terrains of the frontiers began in the form of explorations. But the initial exploration by administrators was followed mainly by anthropological research. The company entrusted Francis Hamilton (later known as Buchanon Hamilton) and R. B. Pemberton to prepare reports on the provinces of the frontiers of Bengal. After the annexation of Assam, the officers serving in Assam were required to prepare reports on the frontier tribes and the officers of the Company, both civil and military, sent their exploratory reports on tribal life and organisations, although biased in most cases[3] to the government. The proselytising objectives of the Christian missionaries to venture out to this new region did not bear any substantial result except those in the Mishmi Hills in 1835 (Mishmis live in the north-eastern part of the state) and the Abor Hills in 1885 (Abors now called the Adis living in the central part of the state).

The British policy to keep this state away from the purview of general administration got thwarted after the Chinese movement of 1910 on the frontiers. The British now thought it wise to finalise the hitherto unsettled boundary between two countries which resulted in some explorations and survey expeditions into the frontiers. In fact, they never attempted to prepare a co-ordinated account of the different tribes of the frontier region. From 1881 onwards, monographs on the frontier tribes began to be included in the Census of India Reports and by 1947 all but the tribes of the western hills and those who lived on the fringes of the border were covered in these reports. But the reports, statistical data, books and accounts of these tribes written by the British officials proved to be what M. L. Bose, the legend historian puts, incomplete and undependable. Few trustworthy accounts of the time are available in the *Descriptive Ethnology of Bengal* (Calcutta, 1872, 1960) of E.T. Dalton and *Linguistic Survey of India*, Vols. I-IV (Calcutta, 1905) of George Grierson.

Under such background, whatever mass of reports and accounts of any nature related to frontier people placed before the readers, were taken to be elusive, biased, partial and incomplete. Much of these were in the form of notes, articles, essays, reports and monographs; but no comprehensive work including all aspects of the life of the frontier people, their land, economy, history and culture has yet been published. L. N. Chakravarty justifiably puts, "We have practically no material, written or unwritten, relating to the history of this area other than some oral literature and a number of historical ruins lying in the foothills along the territory. Initially, up to 1865, we knew of only three ruins namely, Bhalukpong in the West Kameng district and Tamreswari temple and Bhismaknagar in the Lohit district. But as a result of subsequent explorations and excavations a good number of other such ruins dating approximately from the early Christian era have been brought to light".[4] These ruins, when interpreted tell us about the area being known and inhabited by people having close relation with the rest of the country lying especially to the west.

Whatever little have been discovered so far by the conjoint efforts of various explorers as well as some notable findings in recent times with the progress of archaeological and geological activities in the region require to be properly assessed and brought together. Until up to 1991 no intensive study of the available materials could be brought about. Hence, Subid Chatterjee writes, "An intensive study of the available material from different stand points is imperative in view of the paucity of the relics. An impediment in respect of the reconstruction of the early history of Arunachal lies in the lack of literary tradition among most of the inhabitants of the Province. Besides, there is no readymade example set by experts that may be followed in writing a connected history of Arunachal."[5]

The post- independence era witnessed a number of works on the Frontier, particularly in the wake of the Chinese invasion of 1962 coming out in concern with the border problems and the military issues dominated the official and public thinking. A few books claiming to deal with its history chiefly narrated the policy of the British government towards the tribes of Arunachal. A modest attempt to interpret the archaeological materials was made in *Archaeology in Arunachal Pradesh*, Shillong, 1980 by Y.A. Raikar and S. Chatterjee. But a full-length history of Arunachal Pradesh based on all these materials as well as the comparative study of ethnological and linguistic data and early literary accounts relating to Arunachal, adjoining parts of Assam and the neighbouring foreign territories like Tibet, Bhutan and Myanmar came out in the form of a monograph titled *A Comprehensive History of Arunachal Pradesh* (Calcutta, 1991) by Subid Chatterjee. This being an outstanding effort, the emphasis was laid on the reconstruction of the developments in chronological term and the discovery of cultural ethos prevalent in the region in different periods as far as possible.

Some books exclusively on the North –East Frontier and particular tribes and their institutions and culture were issued from the NEFA Administration during 1958-71 like *The Myths of the North-East Frontier of India* (1958) and *A Philosophy of NEFA* (1959) by Verrier Elwin; *Games of NEFA* (1959) by Marion D. Pugh; *The Art of The North-East Frontier* (1959) by

Verrier Elwin; *The Daflas* (1959) by R. Sinha; *The Tangsas* (1959) by P. C. Datta; *The Idu Mishmis* (1961) by T.K.M. Barua; *The Sherdukpens* (1961) by R.P.R. Sharma; *Democracy in NEFA* (1965) by Verrier Elwin; *Mopin* (1966) by Kumar Ishan; *Hill Miris of Subansiri* (1970) by J.N. Chowdhury; *Constitutional and Administrative Growth of the North- East Frontier Agency* (1971) by Col. P.N. Luthra; *The Adi Religion* (1971) by J.N. Chowdhury and *Glimpses of the History of Arunachal* (1973) by L.N. Chakravarty. The works *like A Philosophy of NEFA* of Verrier Elwin and *Constitutional and Administrative Growth of the North –East Frontier Agency* of P.N. Luthra proved worthy. While the former contained directives to the Agency officials the latter became practically a compendium of the notices published from time to time to specify the Inner Line in particular and the administrative and constitutional provisions for the Frontier Administration after 1914 in general.

Apart from the Agency publications, several others have also been brought out like *India's North- East Frontier in the Nineteenth Century* (1955), *Leaves from the Jungle* (1958), *Hill People of the North- East India* (1959), *The Tribal World of Verrier Elwin* (1964), *Kingdom of the Young* (1968), all of them by Verrier Elwin; J.N. Chowdhury's *Arunachal Panorama* (1973); P. Mehra's *The Macmahon Line and After* (1973) and K. Gupta's *The Hidden History of the Sino-Indian Frontier* (1973) which have enriched significantly the frontier history.

The Present Study

History is truth and truth is history. Both of them stand in continuity with each other. Any attempt of their fragmentation certainly leads to unholy presentation of facts. Periodising history in this context seems to be an unholy attempt. It is an uphill task to periodise Indian History, fixing any particular time for the growth and decline of any historical phenomenon in India rejecting the historical truth that history believes in continuity. But for the sake of convenience, periodisation has been made into Hindu, Muslim and British or more appropriate divisions like Ancient or Early, Medieval and Modern basing upon the history of the Northern India with its geographical thrust on the Ganges Valley.

Generally it is construed that the Ancient period begins with the Harappan Culture from C. 2500 B.C. and ends with C. 1000 A.D. The advent of the Muslims as the most dominating political power in India is accepted as the end of the ancient period and the beginning of the medieval. The year 1757 with Battle of Plassey offering the British a strong footage to hegemonise their political power over Bengal is generally taken as the end of the medieval period and the beginning of the modern one.

Given the parameters of periodisation of Indian History discussed above, the regional history with special reference to the history of Arunachal Pradesh stands apart. Looking at the structure of history of the whole of India such division is not encouraging, because there is no uniform and common date for the establishment of Muslim rule in India. Even the foundation of the British rule which is taken as the beginning of the modern period varies at different regions of India asking the historians to believe in a different period of beginning of the Modern period. It is established that chronology is the only tool by which periodisation of even regional history can be validated. But unfortunately history of Arunachal Pradesh does not have a chronological sequence of historical process and development unlike of the parallels existing with regional history elsewhere in the country which conforms to the aforesaid parameters of periodisation.

To conduct historical research in Arunachal Pradesh is very difficult since materials, written or unwritten, relating to the history of this area other than some oral literature, some historical ruins lying in the foot hills of the territory and a few archaeological remains are practically not available. Initially up to 1865, the scholars knew of only three ruins namely, Bhalukpong in the West Kameng District and Tamreswari temple and Bhismaknagar in the Lohit District. But as a result of subsequent explorations and excavations a good number of other such ruins dating approximately from the early Christian era have been brought to light.

A survey of the prehistoric findings in Arunachal reveals that most of them are exploratory in nature without any stratigraphic context. Only Parsi-Parlo site of the Damin circle in the Lower Subansiri district where some Neolithic tools could be excavated by A. A. Ashraf during 1982-83, gives us an idea of cultural development from a Ceramic Neolithic to Ferrolithic stage. However, various Palaeolithic tools from Daphabhum in the Lohit district discovered by B. P. Bopardikar in 1969-70, single specimen from Pagam in Lower Subansiri area excavated by A. A. Ashraf along with evidence of fossil in Arunachal indicate the existence of Lower Palaeolithic culture here. The discovery of a vertebrate fossil by the geologists in 1974-75 from the Upper Tertiary rocks of Ramghat area in the Lower Subansiri proves to be quite significant in so far as it indicates the continuation of Siwaliks to the Eastern Himalayas or Arunachal Siwaliks. The Upper Tertiary horizon of Arunachal now seems to have been inhabited by Hominid and Palaeolithic men. Their proximity, ecological identity and similarity of remains go to suggest that they belonged to the same ethnic tribes who were also responsible for the contemporary cultures of North East-India, Myanmar, South China and South-East Asian countries.

Despite these excavations no radio-carbon dating has so far been made possible in the region to ascertain the age of the Palaeolithic sites deciphered in some of the regions for their validation in favour of periodisation. Accounts of the Greek travellers to India in early Christian era refer to the land and people of Arunachal Pradesh. Pliny, in his book *Natural History* (first century A.D.) gives an account of the people of the frontier Himalayan regions which gives us an indication that these people were the Tibeto-Burman tribes of northern Assam. Pliny refers to the people like the Syrites, Mandai, the Ornulae, Coribae and the Abali; the Ornulae and Abali being identified as the Akas of West Kameng and Abors (Adis) of East Siang districts of Arunachal Pradesh respectively. The Chinese traveller Yuan Chwang (seventh century A.D.) is said to have mentioned about the Adis of Arunachal, as mentioned by Edward Gait in his book, *A History of Assam*.

Sculptural remains, mainly consisting of religious icons found in the Buddhist gompas, monasteries and chortens (*Stupas*) of Tawang, West Kameng, West Siang and Dibang Valley districts ascribe to the eleventh-twelfth centuries A.D. or still later times. Beautiful icons of Hindu deities discovered from once a gigantic temple at Malinithan in the West Siang district, built of stones and compared to temples of India particularly those in Odisha of ninth to twelfth centuries A.D., are variously datable to different periods between the tenth and fourteenth centuries. Inscriptions found within the boundaries of present Arunachal Pradesh so far known do not go beyond fourteenth century A.D. The earliest datable inscription is found from the Tamresvari Temple in the Lohit district written in Sanskrit language and Assamese-Bengali script of the fifteenth century A.D. which throws some light on the political, religious and cultural history of the period.

All these discussions go to suggest that there was no fixed chronological date which could be put into the framework of ancient Indian history of Arunachal Pradesh compared to the historical process taking place in northern India according to which periodisation is made. Arunachal accounts for a varied datable chronology deciphered so far spanning over from palaeolithic culture to fifteenth century A.D. which itself shows both Ancient and Medieval historical occurrences of Arunachal Pradesh within it. There is no definite and significant historical phenomenon occurring in the region which could be taken as a yardstick to differentiate medieval from that of ancient as is the justification in case of periodisation of Ancient and Medieval Indian history. If Ancient history begins with the Harappan Culture from 2500 B.C. and ends up by 1000 A.D. or 1200 A.D. and the Medieval Indian history with the advent of the Muslims as the dominating political power, no such evidences are available so far in Arunachal Pradesh in order to ascertain their contemporaneity with Indian.

If we take Assam as a feeder region with which Arunachal Pradesh had greater accessibility, a different kind of historical mooring emerges in a medieval set-up. Assam comes in contact with the Turko-Afghan rulers of Bengal in the early part of thirteenth century A.D. when the first expedition to Kamarupa during the period of the Delhi Sultanate led by Muhammed-bin-Bakhtiyar Khalji, the Governor of Bihar under Qutb-ud-din Aibak takes place in 1205 A.D. Even then Assam was not conquered and ruled by the Turko-Afghans during the medieval period of her history. Mention may be made that it was a kingdom by the Tai-Shans popularly known as 'Ahoms' getting founded in Assam during the same period which continued from 1228 A.D. to 1826 A.D. Here in case of Assam the advent of Muslims does not play as significant a role as the advent of Ahoms in testifying its corroboration to the criterion for periodisation of medieval Indian history. If it is so with Assam, it was far less with Arunachal Pradesh, practically showing nil influence of the Muslims on its history and politics.

The above discussion shows a complete different historical conjecture in Arunachal Pradesh in comparison to the history of Northern India. Scholars have used different parameters to periodise Indian history. Cultural changes in India in the post-Gupta period which marked the end of all India classical period in the sixth or seventh century A.D. are suggested as the starting of medieval period in Indian history. Further, the post-Gupta period in which certain economic factors played a decisive role such as the feudalisation of state-apparatus through land-grants, gradual decline of trade, monetisation of economy and commodity production, decay of urban centres, rise of local units of production and self-sufficient village economy is taken as transition period from Ancient to Medieval. Techno-economic changes that took place with the foundation of the Delhi Sultanate with qualitative changes on material aspects of Indian culture by the introduction of Persian wheel, mechanism of the handloom, paper production etc. also are taken as the beginning of the medieval period in Indian history. Though the religion of the ruler or the ruling class should not be taken as a criterion for periodisation, there is no doubt that the establishment of Islam as the most dominant political power with major administrative changes in the Indian subcontinent in the twelfth-thirteenth century, marked a turning point in Indian history which signifies the end of the Ancient period and beginning of the Medieval one. Even if we take these parameters it is difficult to periodise the history of Arunachal Pradesh within the above chronological framework.

Moreover, the political and dynastic history is completely missing from the annals of Arunachal history right from the ancient period to the modern with the absence of kingdom and its rule except those of the genealogical and migrational myths of the tribes. It is difficult to trace out the relations of the Arunachal tribes with the outside world prior to the sixteenth century A.D. due to want of any authentic record. Their relations with the Ahom rulers of Assam could only be felt possible as early as 1523 A.D. due to some socio-economic and political interests. One of the key factors which regulated these relations was the tough geography of Arunachal and the lack of some of the daily necessities of life in this area, such as salt, iron and clothes etc. To meet these requirements, they had to depend on the plains. Hence they frequently raided the plains and obtained these articles by force. It was the reason why the Ahom ruler Pratap Singha (1603-1641) introduced the '*Posa*' system as means of compensation to the tribes to protect the subject of the plains from the raids. But significant changes were absent on the basis of which the vital pillars of medieval history could not be constructed.

Even politically and culturally Arunachal Pradesh was still far beyond her modern character up to the early years of India's independence when North India got transformed from her Ancient to Medieval and from Medieval to Modern. Hence, a relevant query comes up here, can we fix 1523 A.D. (whereby first ever Ahom- Arunachal relations in the form of Adi- Ahom relations are justifiably found to be established), as the terminal date for the end of Ancient period and beginning of the Medieval period in the history of Arunachal Pradesh? Similarly, it is difficult to characterise the period from 1523 A.D. to the British relations with Arunachal Pradesh in 1825 (if the British nexus with the tribes which began as early as 1825 is taken as the criterion for the end of medieval period and beginning of the modern period) as the Medieval period.

No doubt, the Ahom-tribal relations brought some socio-economic and political changes in the then Arunachal, but significant changes were absent on the basis of which the historians are constrained to delineate a justifiable line for medieval history.

So far as the British were concerned they developed their relations with the state in different times in different phases. In its Western, Central and Eastern regions they established their relations with different tribes from 1825 to 1838 A.D. (details dealt in the chapters). Hence, the present history of the state is silent about its periodisation given the parameters of periodisation of Indian history. No such work has come up so far delineating the line of periodisation in the history of Arunachal Pradesh even though several papers on the same theme have made inroads generally on the North-East. This work would be of great use while settling the discussion under observation.

Hypothesis Justified

Logical periodisation of the history of the state is expected to bring about fateful disposition of the historical facts avoiding either overlapping or interpolation and encourage the scholars to determinedly put some research findings into its different segments. Instead of three broad divisions of the history of Arunachal Pradesh into Ancient or Early, Medieval and Modern to which it actually never conforms; this history after findings can justifiably be periodised into four sections, i.e. Pre-history, Proto-history, Pre-British and British.

Source Materials Used

The present study is based primarily on published/secondary sources on the history of Arunachal Pradesh. Some of the related published monographs and research papers on the same line either on North-East or main-land states are also browsed to substantiate the study. Extensive study of the local sources and literature pertaining to the theme, critically assessed as to how they could contribute potentially to the study under observation has enlightened the darker areas of the study. The information consulted and collected from the Ph.D. and M. Phil dissertations (both published and unpublished) related to the topic in Rajiv Gandhi University, Itanagar (the only university in the state); North-Eastern Hill University, Shillong; Guwahati University, Guwahati; Dibrugarh University, Dibrugarh and from useful sources available with the Department of History and Antiquarian Studies (DHAS), Guwahati, the premier historical research institute in the region established by the Government of Assam in 1928 having a wide stock of historical sources of the region to its credit like manuscripts, transcripts, rare books on Assam, old chronicles and constructive historical compilations has been objectively studied to find relevance.

Besides, Assam State Museum, Guwahati and Arunachal Pradesh State Museum and Library, Itanagar have been consulted for relevant information in respect of the study. The records and various research publications lying with the Directorate of Research, Government of Arunachal Pradesh, Itanagar have proved of immense help to justify the end. Published materials and Project Reports related to the topic available with historical and social science research institutes in North-East in particular and National Library, Kolkata; National Archives/ National Museum/ ICHR & ICSSR Libraries, New Delhi in general have also been carefully studied to link relevance to Arunachal Pradesh.

Optimistically, the work is expected to open up ideas for threadbare inclusion and synchronisation of different facts into the different segments of history of Arunachal Pradesh and prove to be a useful study on the subject generating interests and inspiration among the scholars and students of history. The study is expected to be a potential source of the periodisation of the history of Arunachal Pradesh.

References

1. S. Dutta (ed), *Studies* in the *History, Economy* and *Culture* of *Arunachal Pradesh,* Itanagar, 2000, p. 147.
2. M.L. Bose, *British Policy in the North- East Frontier Agency*, New Delhi, 1979, p. VII.

3. *Ibid.*
4. L.N. Chakravarty, *Glimpses of the Early History of Arunachal*, Directorate of Research, Government of Arunachal Pradesh, Itanagar, 1995, preface.
5. Subid Chatterjee, *A Comprehensive History of Arunachal Pradesh,* Calcutta, 1991, p. 2.

Chapter - 2

Arunachal Pradesh: An Outline of its History

Arunachal Pradesh (the land of dawn) is located in the extreme north-eastern corner of India. It is bordered by Bhutan on the west, China (Tibet) on the north and north-east, Myanmar on the east and south-east and the states of Assam and Nagaland to its south. Situated at the eastern end of the Himalayas, it is here that the Himalayan range changes its east- west orientation to a north- south one. Much of the southern border follows the foothills bordering the northern fringes of the Brahmaputra Valley. Known in Tibet as the Tsang-po, the great river curves around the Himalayas and enters Arunachal as the Siang. It meets the Lohit, another great river that originates in China, short after it moves into plains and from this union is born the Brahmaputra, the 'Son of God'. Other big rivers- Kameng, Subansiri and Dibang flow into the Brahmaputra, carving out distinctive valleys that form the natural divisions that make up the state.

The state has a territory of 83,743 square kilometre, which is about 2.55 percent of India's land area and a third of the area of North-East India (32.83 percent excluding Sikkim). The largest state in North-East India, the area of Arunachal Pradesh is slightly more than that of Assam but its population is 0.11 percent of India's population. The population density in Arunachal Pradesh is 17 people per square kilometre (2011 Census). This stands in sharp contrast to the population density of 382 per square kilometre in the country. The state has a highly precipitous and varied terrain. Elevations range from 300 meters on the edge of Assam to above 7,000 meters on its northern borders. The land is unparalleled in the world for the concentration, isolation and diversity of tribal cultures it contains. Nowhere else one can find such a patchwork of discrete types of pre-industrial political economics in such a small area, including semi-nomadic swidden agriculture, terraced wet agriculture, high mountain pastoralism and traditional trade and barter system.

Traditionally, the political organisation ranged from aristocratic ranking or stratified chiefdoms to egalitarian clan or lineage-based societies and highly corporate village run by democratic debate in traditional councils. Arunachal Pradesh has ninety-six percent hill terrains and it is the hills which have acted as the natural boundaries for the different communities that inhabit it. Much of the land is forested and the landscape and forests vary from the western end of the state to the east with changing altitude. Rich in a variety of flora and fauna, Arunachal has nourished in its hilly terrains different people, cultures and institutional configurations. Home to 26 major tribes and 110 sub-tribes and minor tribes the state has received waves of migration from different directions over centuries. The early waves were probably form Bhutan, Tibet, Burma (Myanmar) and Yunnan. The more recent migrants are largely form Myanmar and Bangladesh. The mountains kept the various tribal clans isolated from each other and there was not much homogenisation. In fact, each group maintained its own distinct language (and often even a different dialect), belief systems and culture.

The history of Arunachal Pradesh has been constructed largely from oral sources passed down from generation to generation, in verse and song. The Ahom *Buranjis* (Chronicles of the Ahom Kings of Assam) and some archaeological findings that have been unearthed in the area have helped to reconstruct the history. While the land has been inhabited since pre- historic times, it has not come under the direct rule of the British or indeed under the rule of any king in Delhi.

The Ahoms did not rule over the hills of present-day Arunachal Pradesh, but they did maintain contact with the people. Their primary motivation was to protect their empire from depredation by hill tribes and to exercise control over the trade between the regions. Few trade routes passed through the hill tracts to Tibet and China. Occasionally, they undertook a 'show of force' exercise, much as the British did, hundreds of years later. The Ahoms introduced a system of paying 'posa' (literally money) to some tribes to buy peace.

Archaeological finds in Dibang Valley at Rukmininagar and Bhismaknagar, the copper temples at Tamreswari and Parsuramkund in Lohit district, the ruins of the Bhalukpong Fort and the Itafort in Papumpare suggest some contact between the rulers of Assam and the people of Arunachal Pradesh. By 1830s, the British were firmly in control of the Brahmaputra valley. Their approach to the hill people of present-day Arunachal Pradesh was remarkably similar to the policies followed by the Ahoms. By and large the British Empire left the tribes alone, resorting to forays in the form of punitive expeditions only when their commercial and revenue interests were affected. In 1914, the hill areas of the northern districts of Assam were separated to form the North-East Frontier Tracts, which in 1954 became the North-East Frontier Agency (NEFA) with five frontier divisions: the Kameng and Subansiri Frontier Division, the Tirap Frontier Division, the Siang Frontier Division, the Lohit Frontier Division and the Tuensang Frontier Division (which later became a part of Nagaland). The Government of India passed the North-Eastern Areas (Reorganisation) Act, 1971 which gave birth to the Union Territory of Arunachal on January 20, 1972 separating NEFA from Assam. Finally, it got the status of a full-fledged state on February 20, 1986.

History of a particular people is not overnight made. It is made brick by brick. It is the origin and clan structure of the people, their socio- politico- religious- cultural ethos which largely determine the course of history to be written on them. Documentation of all such ethos is an important tool of history.

More is the documentation; merrier is the richness of history. People's contact and exposure with the outside world happens to be dynamic nomenclature to see history growing and gaining momentum. Human history is replete with all such examples. Civilisational habitations, structures, tools used, goods exchanged or traded, engineering and architectural skills, acumenship, entrepreneurship and their subsequent applications leave sufficient cornerstones at respective fields for history to shape leaving apart.

Again, the role of the historian to thread the incidents of history into a form of history is equally significant. History becomes a study of reality in its aspect of becoming. The function of the historian is neither to love the past, nor to condemn the past, nor to be free from the past but to master the past in order to understand its bearing on the present. Historical activity involves three different types of functions which should be performed simultaneously. The first is to set at the truth, to know the entire human past as it actually happened and to be sure that solid facts are at hand. The second job is to interpret the facts, assess and evaluate and explain their significance. The third is to present the ideas in a clear and lucid manner. These three functions make the historian a scientist to gather facts, a philosopher to interpret them and a litterateur to express them. Hence given the discussion held above, the history of the origin of the different tribes needs to be highlighted for a kind of history to be placed before the readers written by a historian that we see and construe as the history of Arunachal Pradesh.

History of the Origin of the Tribes of Arunachal

The origin of the tribes of Arunachal Pradesh is shrouded in mystery. The written history to this account before the advent of the British is not available. Since cent percent illiteracy prevailed among these tribes, they could not write the past history.[1] Moreover, they lived in such inhospitable mountainous terrains that the people from the plains could not establish any contact with them. The history of the tribes whatever known, is based on the tribal tales, palaeolithic tools discovered and anthropological research made by the anthropologists who personally, taking so much of pain, visited and surrounded the area. But tales and researches do not present a clear picture about the origin of the hill tribes living in the North-Eastern Frontier of India. It was the British anthropologists, administrators, surveyors and missionaries who made some sincere efforts and attempts in nineteenth century to discover the identities of these people. But what they discovered and noted about them are mostly concerned with their social, cultural and religious life.

However, some British authors and visitors who personally paid visits to the area and established personal contact with the people threw some light on their origin and migration to this part. But they also produced different views about their origin. Some of them believe that the hill tribes of the North-East India belong to the Indo- Mongoloid race. Some Indian scholars too believe that the tribes living in the hills of North East India primarily belonged to the Indo-Mongoloid group who had migrated to India in the tenth century B.C and confined themselves to the tracts of the North-Eastern Region of India. They also believe that these tribes were originally known as *Kiratas* of India whose description is available in the ancient Indian literatures.[2] Dr S.K. Chatterjee also holds, "The *Kiratas* were known to the Hindu world as a group of people whose original home was in the Himalayan slopes and in the mountains of East, in Assam particularly, who were yellow in colour and presented a distinct type of culture. They had spread all over the plains of Bengal up to the sea".[3]

The modern anthropologists and scholars do not subscribe what Dr S.K. Chatterjee opines that the *Kiratas* were none else than the hill people of the North-East India. But it does not mean that the tales of the Hindu epics are totally baseless and meaningless. It is a fact that Lord Krishna and Balaram as well as the Pandavas had not only visited these areas but also established mutual group cordial relations with the people living in these areas. What is mostly required to substantiate the truth in this regard is to make close and thorough investigations and research to find out the truth mentioned in the Hindu epics in regard to the contact of the people of the plains of India with the hill tribes of North-East India in ancient period.

The Hindu mythologies and religious scriptures throw some light on the relations of the ancient Hindu rulers with the people of Arunachal. It is held that the territory around Sadiya was known as Vidarbha where Pandavas had made their temporary abode during the period of their exile and had established some relations with the hill people. The archaeological relics have been found in the areas in the present day Lohit district of Arunachal which substantiate the truth mentioned in the Hindu religious scriptures. The place Bhismaknagar of Lohit where the archaeological relics have been found indicates that it was the capital of the King Bhismak whose daughter Rukmini who loved Lord Krishna was kidnapped by him when her brother Rukma denied her to marry the Lord. Again, the ruins of a fort at Bhalukpong on the right bank of the river Bharali in the West Kameng district of Arunachal give some account on the mythological tales of the Hindus. The Akas still believe that the original home of their ancestor Bhaluk was at Bhalukpong. Bhaluk was the grandson of king Banasur who got defeated by Lord Krishna at Tezpur. In the Lohit district there are ruins of copper temple known as Tamreswari (name of the Hindu goddess) which gets recognition as a great place of sanctity. There is also the Brahmakund at lower reaches of the Lohit district. It is believed that Parashuram, a renowned Rishi of India, had opened a passage through the hills with a single blow of his axe. It is a great place of pilgrimage even today.

But it is yet to establish whether the hill tribes of the North East India migrated to India either in the late B.C. or in the A.D. The thing which is beyond dispute is that these tribes are the off-shoots of the Indo-Mongoloid race who originally belonged to the non-Chinese Chian tribes of the Central Asia who first came to the North East border of China in late B.C. and later on they spread all over China, Indonesia, Philippines, Bhutan and Burma.[4] This is proved from the fact that these hill tribes bear similarity with some tribal groups as the Dyaks and Koyans of the Indo-Chinese countries. W.C. Smith also holds that the social customs and culture of these Indian tribes resemble with those of the Dyak and the Koyan- the tribes of Indonesia and Philippines. He believes that the hill tribes of North-East India belong to the same blood which is found with the people of Burma and Bhutan.[5]

All these North-Eastern tribes migrated gradually to this part in different groups crossing the mighty Irrawaddy and the Chindwin Rivers of Burma and settled here occupying different hill terrains as per their preferences and conveniences. Some of the tribes such as Caron, Shan, Chin, Singpho, Khampti and Daphla (now changed to Nyishi) etc. who had come from the western China first settled in Burma and Indonesia etc. Getting confronted with inconveniences in the places of their original settlements some of them migrated to the North–Eastern Frontier of India and finally confined themselves to the areas which they are presently occupying. Since the areas they occupied were covered with dense forests and rugged terrains, there could not be held any communication between the people of the plains and the tribes living in these areas.[6]

Being isolated for long and free from any interference from the people of the plains, these people established their respective tiny sovereign village states. Each of the tribes earmarked its territory by raising the boundary lines. Later on, they started their terrace and jhum cultivation. "They established", as Chandrika Singh puts, "their rule on the basis of ancient Greek City State in the sense that a village state contained an organised political community".[7] The customary laws and traditions took the place of their code of conducts. As they remained far from the modern civilisation and confined themselves to isolation, they never managed to "establish a single sovereign state of all the tiny village states"[8]. It is also a fact that due to their migration to the North-East India in separate groups and their confinement to the different ridges covered with dense jungles, each group kept itself aloof from others with the result that variation took place in their respective culture, behaviours, customs, dialects and beliefs.

The reason why these tribal people migrated to this inhospitable and mountainous part of land appears to be the search for their livelihood. Chandrika Singh also points out, "They could have settled in the plains, but the plains area had already been occupied". The only vacant space for them was the hill areas. Therefore, they occupied the area and settled comfortably without any disturbances and interferences. Though the arrival of the Ahoms in the plains of Assam and their firmly established rule disturbed the isolation of those tribes who were living on the lower portion of these hills it could not bring much difference in their internal life. It was the contact of the British with these people which in fact, brought about major changes in the traditional outlook and in political and economic life of the tribal people of the North-East India."[9]

The process of administrative and constitutional development of these tribes started about a century back when the British extended their administration to certain parts of this territory. But it gained momentum only after independence. The story of the politico- administrative development of this area after independence is also a story of a search for and forging of a common personality by an assortment of people belonging to a number of tribes brought together by accident of history. At the time of independence other states and territories of India had their own identity developed through many decades or even centuries. Arunachal however, consisted of three artificially created administrative units, namely, the Balipara Frontier Tract, the Sadiya Frontier Tract, and the Tirap Frontier Tract loosely administered by the British before independence as "Excluded Areas" under the Government of India Act, 1935. Each one of them was inhabited by a number of tribes or tribal groups having nothing in common except geographical proximity and ethnic similarity. Some of them were even antagonistic to each other. After independence the administration of these "Excluded Areas" passed on to the hands of Government of Assam but no change was brought in the quality of administration except for bifurcation of the Sadiya Frontier Tract into two districts of the Abor (Adi) Hills and the Mishmi Hills in 1948.

Situation of Arunachal Pradesh at that time presented a picture of a hilly terrain devoid of developed means of communication with a sparse population cut up into numerous isolated tribes or village communities. The people were mostly suspicious of outsiders like any other tribal people. The British had considered the area too backward and unrewarding for extending any civil administration there. The socio-political life of the tribes of the area therefore were untouched by any modernising influence and remained primitive till the early years of independence of India.[10]

Trends of Socialisation

Migration of these tribes to the present state of Arunachal and their subsequent settlement at different places led to the growth of different socio-economic, political and cultural ethos to determine the process of socialisation among them. Otherwise, given the diversity and insularity of the tribes the present day Arunachal bears, the state could have been dissipated much earlier, unlike the migration of the Aryans in the northern and the Dravidians in the southern India respectively. But the irony is that Arunachal does not breast as much bulky a history as the north or south India has. Geography has played a great role in projecting enormously misbalanced weight of history across the country. Arunachal is certainly a victim of that. Much of its history has grown upon its people's social organisation, political institutions, religious and cultural traditions. It is pertinent to know about them for associating them with the kind of history that should have been grown up as we suppose to have been given the parameters of history to include them in its different phases.

If man is a social animal, the term 'social' can be defined to represent those qualities that render a man useful in the society and make him fit for human intercourse. Aristotle puts,

"Man is fated to live in a society and he needs other men in order to fulfil his spiritual essence". This opinion holds good even today, particularly in case of Arunachal where the issue of interdependence on one another was much more felt than in most other parts of the country. Again, the culture of any people is a synthesis of the aspects of their social, educational, religious, artistic, economic and other activities and is a product of the struggle of mankind against the natural as well as manmade forces of the modern day. Convenience for methodology has led to the classification of culture as primitive, medieval or modern culture and the tribal culture of Arunachal has often been termed as primitive; the society as backward. This seems to be absolutely incorrect if we take the opinion of T.C. Hudson into account where he goes to say "The lower culture, in fact, is the basis of human societies".

One more opinion goes to say that the tribal society has changed little if at all over hundreds of years. This stands again incorrect. There remains no doubt that there had been a steady evolution of the tribal society and culture over the years. Further, the tribes of this region have another inheritance from the Mother Nature itself- the land and its climate. No study on the history of Arunachal can be said complete without keeping in mind the tough landscape and the extreme climate of this area that have shaped the society of the people. Due to absence of outside assistance the people learnt to co-operate by organising themselves into very cohesive village communities, which were in most of the cases, under a committee of locally respected elders, to care for almost every need of the people. Thus, while trying to study the history and historiography of Arunachal, basing their society and culture as tools, we should not skip in our mind the tribal enduring, inheritance of climate, land and the fact that this region remained mostly cut away from the mainstream of the Indian society till very recently.

Standing isolated from the rest of the world for centuries and faced with extremely difficult living conditions, the tribes of this area have created a realistic picture of life as they face it with all its hardships in their religion. Dr Verrier Elwin, in his book *A Philosophy for NEFA,* has pointed out five outstanding qualities of the religious system of NEFA. Firstly there is a very general belief in a Supreme God who is just, benevolent and good; secondly, in the tribal religion there is a genuine emphasis in the spiritual realities behind the events of everyday life; thirdly, the tribal religion is built from an elaborate mythology; fourthly, the tribal religion is associated with a social ethic that unites the tribe in its discipline and finally, the tribal religion gives the people the power to reconcile themselves in the eternal emergencies of life. We can add one more quality to it, i.e., unlike many other religions of the world, the tribal religion is not a separate institution in itself controlled by a particular section of the society. Their religion is a part of their everyday life, not confined to the shrines or temples only. It has simple ethical codes that unite the people and inspire the tribal qualities of hospitality, simplicity, truthfulness and integrity.

The tribes are now conveniently placed into three cultural groups. The first group includes the tribes like the Nyishis, the Hill Miris, the Apatanis, the Adis, the Galos and the Mishmis who fall in the category of what has been termed as hereditary- Shamanism having many cultural traits and beliefs including their pantheon of gods and spirits in common. The second group consists of the tribes like the Monpas, the Sherdukpens, the Singphos, the Khamptis, the Membas and Khambas who come under the influence of Buddhism and their religious life is deeply influenced by this religion. The third group comprises the tribes like the Noctes, the Wanchos and the Tangsas of the Tirap region who are related to the Naga tribes to their south-west. The religion of the tribes falling in this category can be broadly termed as animism.

How history peeps through social trends?

The social organisation of this tribes hinges around their social activities, relation and behaviour. It is visible through their social institutions like family, marriage, clan and the dormitory system. The smallest unit of the society is the family consisting of father, mother and their children. Mixed extended families are common in most of the communities. However, nuclear and vertically and horizontally extended families are found too. When a family breaks up, custom demands that either the youngest or the eldest son continues living in the parental house to support the family and his old parents. Sometimes, even after marriage, other sons stay on with the parents till they have two or three issues. All members of family living in the same household take their meals from a common hearth. The food is cooked by the mother or by the wife of the eldest son if the mother is too old.

History on property related matter deals something different compared to others in the other part of the country. All movable and immovable property such as cultivate land, bamboo groves, palm leaves, gardens, livestock, granaries, utensils and ornaments are held commonly by the family. The father who happens to be the head of the family is the sole owner of the property, though other members can also show their attachment to it. The authority over the property lies with the father and is inhabited by the eldest or youngest son or by all sons equally after his death. The women have no claim over family property except the articles given to them when they get married. Polyandrous families are prevalent among the Buddhist communities like the Monpas. The societies in Arunachal Pradesh are patrilineal and the people reckon relationship through the male line. But an analysis of their kinship reveals that their system of kinship terminology is a classificatory one, where they recognise the cognate persons as well as affine relationship.

Clans denoted by local category form the utmost criterion of the tribes. Some of the communities have sub-clans, for example, the Tangsas. The Tangsa clans are not connected with totemic objects, but they are ancestral clans. Each tribe traces its descent from a single ancestor, a semi-mythical figure. The subsidiary ancestors are the founders of district clans. The clan's function is to regulate the marriage system. Clan endogamy is considered to be a heinous crime and traditionally punishable. Generally, the clans continue for a period of seven generations or more till, perhaps, due to migration or over population, they split collaterally. This gives rise to sub-clans. The clans and sub-clans are exogamous in the past, among the Adis the settlement pattern of the villages depended on the distribution of clans. Traces of this pattern are noticeable among the Singphos. The social organisation of the Noctes is greatly influenced by the traditional chieftainship system. Two distinct classes are found among them- the chief and his kinsmen form one class while the commoners form the others. Within these two main classes there are different clans. Like the Noctes, the social organisation of the Wanchos is governed by a traditional chieftainship system. There are four classes in their society in descending order -Wangham (the chiefs), Wangesa (the small chief), Wangsu (the intermediate class) and Wangpan (the commoners).

History of Arunachal Pradesh reflects that the tribes allow a lot of freedom to young boys and girls who can mix freely with each other without any reservation, provided they observe the rules of clan exogamy. The boys and girls of the different clans select their friends freely and meet each other generally in the place where young girls sleep. The unrestricted mixing helps them in selecting their life partners. Tribes are basically endogamous, but clan, phratry or moiety exogamy is the fundamental and basic rule of marriage. Intra-clan marriage is considered a serious crime. If anyone violates this rule he or she will not only be excommunicated but also be exterminated by the society, except in the case of the Lisus.[11]

Marriages are generally confined to the same or particular villages. Monogamy is the general rule, but polygamous marriages are prevalent among the chiefs of the Noctes and Wanchos. Some cases of polyandrous marriages are found among the Monpas and some other sections of the Buddhist communities. Mostly negotiated and love marriages prevail among the communities of Arunachal. There is no fixed age of marriage. Sororate and levirate marriages are also prevalent. Bride price is a common practice among the tribals and is generally paid in kind. Divorce is allowed on payment of a fine and both the partners have the right to seek divorce. This is prevalent among the Noctes, Wanchos and most of the Tangsa sub-groups, Adis and Mishmis.

The dormitory provides a place to learn the art of living in an informal manner. It gives an opportunity to young married boys and girls for courtship prior to selecting a life partner. Among the Singphos, when the girl attains puberty she is segregated from the family. She is then provided with a separate room called *pinta- khak* in the house. The girl's dormitory is always situated towards the end of the house so that the girl and her friend may enter without being noticed by any member of the family. Among the Noctes, the boy's dormitory is called *pang*, but the girl's dormitory is very rare, though not unheard of. The Wancho grown-up boys sleep in dormitory called *morung*. There is no separate dormitory for the girls, but they sleep in the house of widows who do not have blood relations with the former. Each Wancho village has several morungs for boys.

So far the Adis are concerned the *moshup* (bachelor's dormitory) plays a significant role as important institution. It is not only a training centre for all practical purposes but also the centre and upholder of cultural traits. The institution is called by different names by the different sub- group of the Adis. The Minyongs call it *dere,* the Padams term it *moshup* and the Milangs and other allied groups call it *ngaptek*. The Boris and Ashings call it *bango*. The *moshup* is usually constructed in the centre of the village from where different approaches to it can be watched and guarded. It is used as a sleeping house by all young men from the age of ten till they take wives to their homes. There are a number of *merums* (fire places) in a *moshup*. Each *merum* is under the supervision of a senior boy who is responsible for the maintenance of discipline in his *merum* and is empowered to punish any defaulter. The *moshup* is used for different types of meetings, especially those of the *Kebang* (a legal and judicial institution at the village level). They are also used for different feasts and festivals. During some festivals girls are allowed to dance inside the *moshup*.

The Adis have a dormitory for girls called *rasheng*. It is a small hut with only one square room with a fireplace in the centre. The adolescent and unmarried girls of the village sleep in their respective clan *rasheng*. These remain unoccupied during the day as the girls return to their respective houses early in the morning. Like the *moshup*, each *rasheng* is under the supervision of a senior and experienced girl and is the training institution for spinning, wearing, dancing, singing and discipline. Young boys from different *moshup*s come and join the girls in the *rashengs* at night and mates are selected in the process. In Adi society marriage succeeds the way the boys and girls select themselves as life partner during their stay in the *moshup* and *rasheng*. Hence, matrimony is a great phenomenon taking place within the jurisdiction of both *moshup* and *rasheng*.

One outstanding feature of the Arunachalee society is the absence of the caste system. Of course, there are social distinctions in many tribes and their society is divided into the nobles or chiefs, priests, the middle class, the slaves or servants and normally, inter-marriage between them is permitted. But this division is more horizontal in nature than vertical. All people in every tribe dine together on social occasions and take part in the village councils. And unlike the caste- system, the social division does not at all jeopardise the social solidarity of the village. Aura of cultural and traditional diversities in the state is a truth incredible without personal experience. Even if globalisation has made its inroad deeper into the dynamism of the culture, traditionality is still in vogue. Even now, there is a considerable prevalence of the primitive subsistence economy. Multi-prong initiatives taken now at the community level to uphold such traditionality prove to be necessary challenges to globalisation. Thanks to the administrative policy of what is called 'let alone', that is, to leave the tribes to themselves[12] adopted by the British government which left the tribal indigenous traditions untouched. The subsequent Indian governments followed the suit without harming the traditionality of the region. Even the Ahoms in Assam (1228-1826 AD) never made any attempt to annex the territory of these tribes, nor did they interfere with their internal affairs.[13] Efforts of the elders of the state to bequeath the traditions from one generation to other signify a strong sense of bond and concern towards their traditions to be kept alive.

The cultural diversity of the people differs from tribe to tribe even if they reside within the same geographical area. The district West Kameng can be taken for an instance. It is the abode to five different tribes- Monpas, Sherdukpens, Akas, Mijis and Buguns who live in close proximity with each other (the distance between two individual habitats cannot even be maximum more than ten kilometres away from each other). But their traditional culture with regards to their religious practices, dress, customs, rituals, languages, dialects, fairs and festivals is starkly different. Traditional Monpa male attire includes a maroon or black *shuba* or *todung* (cloak), *aliphudung* (jacket), *dornath* or *dorna* (trousers) and *khutung/ gamu/chitpa jambo* (cap made of yak hair). A woman's dress consists of a maroon, red or white *todung*, a red or maroon *sinka* (gown) and a waist belt called *mukhok* or chhudang.[14] While the attire of a Sherdukpen living geographically proximate to the Monpas, includes a *sapay* or *endi-chadar* (shawl) diagonally covering the upper part of the body with a *koyok* or *lidik* (a full-sleeve jacket) worn over it and a *mukhok* (waist belt). Further, a *dao* (a machete in a scabbard) is usually attired. A woman wears the *sinka* (white cotton or silk gown).[15] While the Monpa man cuts his hair in a straight line just above the eyes and at the level of the nape behind his neck, his Sherdukpen counterpart prefers to have cropped hair with a skull cap- the *gurdam* (made of yak hair with short tassel like projections jutting down from the sides) to cover it.

History shows, some of the tribes of Arunachal Pradesh practised a hierarchical ordering of different classes or segments of society. However, this class division did not create any complication whatsoever in the tribal society. The social distinctions were hardly noticeable in the ordinary course of life and did not hamper the harmony of society. The concept of untouchability was absent. The relations between the upper classes and lower classes were found to be harmonious. Amongst the Adis of the Siang district, for instance, at one time slaves were found. But there was no custom for keeping the slaves away from the society. The slaves and the masters used to share the same dining hall.[16] The social relations were determined mostly by clan rules. The present position of women in the society runs parallel to the position of women in other parts of rural India. However, there are certain marked differences, the most outstanding being the practice of premarital laxity and freedom of choice of partner. This is a non- Aryan system which is characterised by an ancient institution called communal barracks or bachelor's quarters and is to be found not only amongst the tribes of Arunachal but in many ancient tribes all over the world.

The system of slavery as social institution had considerable value in the traditional Arunachal society. The slaves were labourers in the field, helpers in the house and soldiers in warfare. They were considered as living property of the masters and were often treated as medium of exchange. Salt, cattle and other items could be bartered against them. They could be presented as a token of friendship to others and were also given as bride price as well as dowry. The British Government tried to free the slaves from their masters. After independence, the Government of India also took various measures for the abolition of slavery in the state. Extensive propaganda was also carried out against slavery. The people were asked to regard any child born to a slave after independence as free. Sometimes the slaves themselves were persuaded to collect the money and to purchase their freedom with the assistance of the government and the village council. Slavery by law got abolished from this area in 1960.

How does history peep through polity-trends?

Pre-independent Arunachal had a different phase of her political atmosphere. Communicational handicaps and mountainous terrains compelled the tribes to remain confined to them. Extremely difficult living conditions had made the tribes suspicious of the outsiders. The British never paid any attention to this area and did not extend their civil administration to this land. The political life of the people was thus, village or tribe oriented. Every aspect of life in the village was corporate in character involving joint decision and actions. Every community had a traditional socio-political organisation which governed the life within the community according to traditional laws. Each community loved its own political organisation and functioned as a little independent state. Thus every tribe had its own type of village council or village organisation.

The village organisation or village council prevalent in Arunachal could be classified into five different categories. They were; (1) the Adi republican type where the village solidarity was stronger than the clan or tribe loyalty; (2) the Nocte and Wancho type where one paramount chief had a number of villages with subordinate chiefs under him; (3) the individualistic Mishmi type where the household and the clan formed the basis of a unit; (4) the Monpa theocracy where a number of villages, who were autonomous in internal affairs were interlaced together under the theocratic rule of a monastic authority and (5) the Apatani type where a large village was divided into clan sections, each administered by its own clan council. It must be noted here that the jurisdiction of these different organisations was confined to their respective village or tribe implying the fact that the political perspective of each community was confined to itself. Thus politically, Arunachal Pradesh was a conglomeration of innumerable autonomous communities with varying socio-political ideas and institutions and not a single unit politically, culturally or administratively.

The Indian Constitution brought about change to these areas. The national leaders took deep interest in these areas and formulated careful policy for socio- economic and political development with least interference in the traditionality of the tribes. Hence, the politico- administrative change and development of the area was slow and cautious in the beginning but gained rapidness after catching imagination of the local people. The first major administrative change in the area was effected in 1954 when the NEFA was created bringing all the areas of Arunachal Pradesh under one administrative authority thus giving them a common political identity. The NEFA Administration meticulously followed the policies laid down by the national leaders. It did not allow free flow of outside influences into the area and allowed the hill tribes of Arunachal to continue with their traditional socio-political life. It even encouraged the traditional village councils to develop further. Politics and plans were formulated at the Agency level but their implementation was made community-wise.

Popular participation in the administration was extremely limited and confined to village level. Beyond the village level the channels of association were at Gaon Burahs (village headmen) and Interpreters. The administration therefore remained physically and psychologically away from the people. Each tribe or community still continued to think and work for it. Their political outlook still remained village or tribe oriented. The agency was one single unit at the level of administration only. Philanthropically the administration tried to identify itself with the people and establish mutual trust and understanding. Nothing was done in a hurry and nothing was even imposed or enforced. Respecting their traditional ethos, new ideas and ideals were held up only when the people raised their desirability and themselves adopted them. This patience and perseverance paid great dividends in terms of transforming a number of assorted tribal communities into a comparatively cohesive political unit. A new consciousness for change and progress came into being. The hills started changing towards a common goal.

Time passed by. It was felt necessary for the organisation of a higher level of association for fostering larger and wider political consciousness. The Chinese aggression of 1962 hastened this line of thinking and a sense of urgency was felt to bring Arunachal Pradesh too into the mainstream of national political life. A committee to study the possibility of the introducing the modern Panchayat Raj on the lines of the rest of the country was appointed in 1964 so that a uniform political system could be introduced throughout the territory under the chairmanship of late Dr Daying Ering. On the recommendation of this Committee and on the basis of the North-East Frontier Panchayat Raj Regulation, 1967, which embodied them, a system of Panchayat Raj bodies was constituted in the entire territory in 1969- the Gandhi Centenary year. An Agency Level popular body, the Agency Council was linked with the Panchayat bodies for the first time and was inaugurated in December 1969 at Shillong.

Henceforth, modern political processes to the Territory were brought in which greatly influenced the traditional political institutions of the tribes of this area. It introduced a graded series by which village leadership could mount up through Anchal and District to the Agency level of association in policy making and planning. At the top, the local leadership had to view the entire territory as one, though it was directly concerned with its own district. The indirect elections promoting leaders from the lowest and smallest to the highest level trained them to get over their limitation of localised interest and develop at least a district perspective. In the Agency Council each district had to take cognizance of the others and to think in terms of the Agency as whole. It is at this stage that the communities got less mentioned compared to district level planning and deliberations. The Agency here could be felt as an integrated political unit and not as a mere package of assorted communities.

Birth of the Panchayat Raj ushered a new orientation in the politics of Arunachal Pradesh which was embedded in the small group 'psyche'. It broadened the political horizon of the people asking them to look beyond their community and it too brought them closer to the Administration filling the gap between the Agency and the village. The political outlook of the local leaders changed and they started thinking in terms of district and the territory instead of the village, community or the tribe. A set of new state level leadership was created through higher level Panchayat bodies. The traditional tribal political institutions continued to function side by side but they too underwent a change under the modernising effects of the Panchayats. They imbibed more and more rational elements in their functions. The new concepts of election, representation, majority decisions etc. slowly started coming into these institutions. The leadership of these traditional institutions also underwent changes and the newly emerging young educated leadership started gaining influence even in the traditional institutions.

Political growth of the territory set in motion new developments in quick succession. The process of political cohesion started by the Panchayats was further strengthened in 1972 when the NEFA was made into the Union Territory of Arunachal Pradesh. The *defacto* political individuality of Arunachal Pradesh carefully developed through all these years got the *dejure* recognition among the several states and Union Territories of the country. Normal political processes of the nation, however, were yet to be extended to the area. Its apex body was still known as Territorial Council and the popular representative nearest to policy making were the Councillors. The territory got its first Legislative Assembly and the first Council of Ministers when the existing Territorial Council was converted into the Legislative Assembly of Arunachal Pradesh in 1975. So far the General Elections were not conducted in the state and the parliamentary representation from the state was through a nominee of the President of India.

The constitution of the Legislative Assembly and the formation of a responsible ministry paved the way for extension of modern elections. In the Parliamentary Elections held in 1977, Arunachal Pradesh was called upon to elect its representatives to the Lok Sabha. Thus, the modern democratic processes of election, secret ballot and adult franchise that were held back for so long in order not to upset traditional life were introduced into the territory. In these elections Arunachal Pradesh retained one of its representatives unopposed while the other was elected by poll. A year later, elections for the State Legislative Assembly were held and the entire territory went to the polls. Arunachal Pradesh was granted statehood on 20th February 1987. Thus the state represents a case of deliberate political socialisation in a very short span of time. Within three decades a primitive tribal society consisting of a number of heterogeneous tribes with their respective traditional socio- political institutions got transformed into a modern set of participatory politics and democratic means of electing their legislators.

British Colonial Interest in the State

The history of Arunachal Pradesh was largely influenced by the twin interests of the British, i.e., colonial interest in the Brahmaputra Valley and imperial commercial interest beyond the frontiers. The process of economic and political incorporation of the Arunachal hills had started with the extension of the British rule in the valley. While the former was manifested mainly through a change in the nature and extent of frontier trade, the latter through the establishment of the British political supremacy and colonial legitimacy. Apart from interest on tea[17], the discovery of coal and petroleum in 1825 in the valley and subsequent development of mining and extraction activities- all these had attracted a huge investment of capital which had been the monopoly of the European merchants and demanded security from the turbulent tribal communities surrounding the valley. But the tea- planters' influence in the valley was so strong that the civil and military elements stood subservient to the interests of them.[18]

On the other hand, the geo-economic importance of the frontier having boundaries with Tibet, Burma (Myanmar) and

Bhutan lured the British to expand their imperial commercial sway towards the Central Asia. There were numerous passes in the Himalayas and Patkai ranges which were being used by different tribal communities of this frontier for trading with Tibet and Myanmar respectively since time antiquity. The East India Company had a long cherished desire to establish trade relations with Tibet which was supposed to be the store-house of gold and specie.[19] Bogle, who had been sent to Tibet by Warren Hastings in 1774 to open a mutual and equal communication of trade, reported that in exchange of Chinese goods the returns are made in gold, pearls, corals, shells, broad cloth and a trifling quantity of Bengal cloth.[20] Since the flow of Tibetan gold and specie in Bengal was drastically declined after the Gurkha conquest of Newar States of Kathmandu, Bhatgaon (presently Bhaktapur) and Patan (presently Lalitpur) during the sixties of 18th century which had been playing the intermediary role in trade between Tibet and Gangetic plains, the Company had to suffer continuous depletion in its reserves of gold and bullions required to finance its Chinese tea-trade. The British annexation of Assam in 1826 not only ushered a new hope to establish trade relations with Tibet through North- Eastern Frontiers but also to look out for Chinese market for the British goods via Burma (Myanmar).

The frontier was found neither congenial for the British colonial interest in the valley nor hopeful for its commercial interest beyond the frontier. As most of the tribes bordering the frontier worked as mediator in the trans- Himalayan trade there was no easy path for the British to make their commercial dream into reality. Moreover, there were constant inter- tribal as well as intra- tribal internecine warfare either for the possession of trading routes of for dislodging the quarrelling opposition from its benefits. The British had then two options either to bring the whole frontier under the British Indian Empire or to remove the ethnocentric barriers of both frontier and trans- frontier trade leaving the frontier tribes to play the intermediary in favour of the Raj. As the first proposition proved very costly for an uncertain future gain, the Company opted for the second.

The colonial legitimacy of the British Indian empire was recognised by the Sherdukpens of western Arunachal in 1826 while their chiefs, popularly called 'Sat Rajahs', came to agreement with the former.[21] The Akas submitted in 1888 while both the Kapaschor Aka Chiefs Medhi and his brother Chandi surrendered before the Deputy Commissioner of Darrang.[22] The Nyishis of Charduar in Darrang came to settlement in 1835 and other clans followed them shortly.[23] Among the Adis, Minyongs were the first to come to agreement with the British in 1862. Other Adi clans also came to terms with the British power by 1866.[24] But it took a long time to completely subdue the mighty Adis. It was only after the Adi expedition of 1911 that had been launched following the murder of Williamson and Gregorson along with their party that the British Government could establish its supremacy over them. The revolt of the Singphos was suppressed in 1843[25] and that of the Khamptis in 1849.[26] In case of the Mishmis, though one Idu Mishmi chief named Kalood went under the British protection in 1868, it was not before 1920 that the final victory came to the British with the death of Pongon, the other Idu Mishmi rebel chief in an encounter with the British army led by Mr O'Callaghan.[27] In all practical purpose all these cut- off years may be deemed as the tentative dates at which the different tribal communities had finally been brought under colonial subjugation following a series of events of action and reaction of both sides.

Hence, by the early Twentieth century, the British had succeeded largely to establish their political supremacy and colonial legitimacy among the hill tribes of the frontier. A few tribes were even brought under direct rule. Permanent administrative centres had been established at Pasighat and Nizamghat (shattered during the 1950 earthquake). During 1917-18 all the Khamptis were assessed to poll tax and treated as full- fledged British subjects.[28] In 1941 a permanent Assam Rifles outpost was established at Rupa and during 1945-46

Sherdukpens, Monpas and some Khowas (Buguns) were brought under tax network (House Tax).[29] In fact, with the delineation of Inner Line in 1873 and Mc Mahon Line in 1914, the tract lying between these two lines roughly corroborates the area of the present day Arunachal Pradesh, the process of political incorporation of the Arunachal hills into the British Indian empire took a definite shape which facilitated the quick political integration of the frontier with independent India.

How do sources speak on history of the state?

When we start to study the history of Arunachal Pradesh we find scant written record available. Absence of a script among the tribes inhabiting the region has been a major drawback for documenting aspects of tribal life for their presentation before the readers in black and white. The history of the region, hence, becomes all the more patchy and fragmented. But the written record has not been the only source of seeking information about the progress and development of the mankind- the subject matter of history. No doubt, there are certain handicaps in reconstructing the history of Arunachal Pradesh; yet there are a number of sources that help us to a considerable extent to draw an account of the area. Why not are all these sources discussed here?

The sources of history of Arunachal Pradesh may be broadly divided under two categories: (A) Archaeological and (B) Literary.

(A) Archaeological Sources

Archaeological sources found in Arunachal are not as varied in nature as we find in other areas. Natural hazards like nature of the soil, frequent landslides, earthquakes, heavy rains and floods, have significantly eroded the archaeological relics of the state. To precipitate this, conducting of frequent archaeological surveys has not been made possible owing to the unfavourable climate of North-East India, with its torrents of rain and frequent occurrence of seismic disturbances. The amount of such sources found in the state is handy which also helps largely in reconstructing its history. So such sources may again be sub- divided into (i) Prehistoric and Stone Age Culture (ii) Excavations (iii) Inscriptions (iv) Coins and (v) Monuments.

Prehistoric and Stone Age Culture

The prehistoric age can be divided into three broad phase (i) Palaeolithic or Early Stone Age (ii) Mesolithic or Middle Stone Age (iii) Neolithic or New Stone Age . The study of the prehistoric archaeology in the region of Arunachal Pradesh was initiated in the later part of the nineteenth century A.D. John Lubbock, one of the pre-historians reported in 1867 a light green Jade Celt, collected by Captain E.H. Steel from Namsang in Tirap region of the eastern Arunachal. In 1870, Captain Steel continued his investigation and was successful in discovering three more Celts from the same area. One of these Celts was of greenish Jade stone, the second of the same material, but smaller in size and the third of a soft white stone, having brownish yellow in its outline. From 1871 to 1937 a lot of tools made of Jadeite of various nature could be deciphered from the Mishmi hills; Sadiya frontier zone, well within present day Arunachal; Mebo in the Siang district; Ningru north of Neo- Dihing river in the Tirap district: Tigra in the Abor hills. Almost all these tools are preserved in the Pitt Rivers Museum, Oxford. It is the work "Prehistory and Proto-history in Eastern India" of Professor A.H. Dani published in 1960 which for the first time reported of such collection.[30]

The study of these tools suggests that as the rock Jadeite was not locally available, these implements reached probably from North Burma or China. The rest of the implements are made on a variety of locally available rocks such as sandstone, schist, basalt, gneiss and talc. Technologically, these implements are identified as: (i) Chipped and edge ground axes: (ii) pecked and edge ground tools and (iii) fully ground tools. This collection speaks two different types. The first one is stone-axes with lenticular cross section and the other one being quadrangular type with rectangular cross section. The minor types are identified as hog backed type of Celt and slender chisel of Jadeite. This collection of stone-age antiquities, besides revealing Neolithic artefacts, also gives an idea of Mesolithic tools of Hoabinhian tradition from Arunachal Pradesh and Nagaland.[31] (The term Hoabinh culture was first used by French archaeologists working in Northern Vietnam to describe Holocene period archaeological assemblages excavated from rock shelters. The related English adjective Hoabinhian (French *hoabianien*) has become a common term in the English-based literature to describe stone artifact assemblages in South-east Asian sites like Terengganu, Sumatra, Thailand, Laos, Myanmar and Cambodia that contain flaked, cobble artifacts, dated to C. 10,000–2000 BCE. The term was originally used to refer to a specific ethnic group, restricted to a limited period with a distinctive subsistence economy and technology).

Further, two shouldered axes from the Singpho and Aka areas could be reported by N. Sarkar between 1962 and 1964. He also collected three chisels, ten complete axes and four broken pieces of axes from different parts of Arunachal. S.N. Rao of Dibrugarh University is said to have detected some objects from the Kamlang Valley of Lohit district which appear to be palaeolithic. In 1972, Professor M.C. Goswami and his associates published a report of a collection of eighteen Neolithic Celts from the Kameng district of Arunachal. Stone Age tools and artifacts along with neoliths and river terraces have been recorded by B. P. Bopardikar of the Archaeological Survey of India in his report of exploration in the Daphabhum area of the Lohit district in 1969-70. This is taken to be the first ever scientific survey done for prehistoric remains of Arunachal with a view to trace the habitation sites of primitive men and to determine relations between western and earthen Himalayan glacial and glaciofluvial phenomena and formation of the terraces of the Stone Age industries.

As a sequence to this exploration, river sections and terraces were detected at Chowkham, Alubari, Hawai, Wakro, Chambe, Kale, Teehun, Glow and Chakhro. Pre-historic antiquities were found only in three sites, viz., Kale, Teehun and Glow in the form of stone age artefacts like cleavers, ovates, chisels, cores, flakes, points, choppers, hand- axes and scrapers, all representing the pre-Neolithic phase of stone age culture in Arunachal Pradesh. One unificial chopper and a flake collected from the lowest terrace at Tawling recalls a similar unificial quartzite chopper type of Kangra valley in Himachal Pradesh. These tools were highly rolled and weathered and mainly obtained from the patches of Jhum fields on the slopes on the terraces. Most of the stone artefacts were made on metamorphic rock, such as meta-dolerite gneisses, quartzite, limestone and schist, which are of the common rock types of the area.

Y. A. Raiker collected chips of semi-precious stones like chalcedony, jasper etc. from Vijayanagar of the Tirap district in 1971, and indicated possibility of getting more microliths on the valley of Neo-Dihing river. He also noticed three triangular ground axes and one bar type polished broken Celt during excavation at Bhismaknagar in the Lohit district without stratigraphic context, now being preserved in the Jawaharlal Nehru State Museum, Itanagar. D. K. Duarah has also discovered a Neolithic site at Parsi- Parlo area of the Damin circle in the Lower Subansiri region. The Neolithic site at Parsi-Parlo excavated during 1982-83 by A. A. Ashraf reveals a single culture period though he has identified three phases, namely Aceramic Neolithic phase, Ceramic Neolithic phase and Ferrolithic phase.

A survey of all such pre-historic findings in Arunachal reveals that most of the finds are exploratory in nature, without any stratigraphic context. Only Parsi- Parlo site gives us an idea of culture development from a Ceramic Neolithic to Ferrolithic stage. However, various palaeolithic tools from Daphabhum and single specimen from Pagam in Lower Subansiri area along with evidence of fossil in Arunachal indicate the existence of Lower Palaeolithic Culture here. In 1974-75 first ever vertebrate fossils, viz., the molar of *Bos* has been unearthed by the Geological Survey of India from the upper tertiary horizon of Eastern Himalayas, in the

Ramghat area of the Lower Subansiri within Arunachal Pradesh. This discovery is of considerable importance, establishing the continuation of the Western Siwaliks, where similar finds are noticeable, bearing similar palaeo-environs. Thus the upper tertiary horizon of Arunachal can be recognised like the Western Siwaliks, as the probable habitation of the area of the Hominids and Palaeolithic man.

Most of the stone tools recovered from the state show Neolithic features. Though various Neolithic implements are noticed, pottery of the period is very few. Only one site Parsi-Parlo has yielded a few potsherds from stratified deposits, revealing its affinity with Chinese and South East Asian pottery. Comparative study of materials and technology exhibits close affinity of the neoliths of Arunachal with the objects of Assam, Burma, Indo-China, China and Malay Peninsula. No proof of iron or copper age culture in Arunachal has so far been made. The combined evidence of ethnology and archaeology, i.e., a clear correlation between a particular type of Neolithic Celt viz., the shouldered and polished variety with Austro-Asialitic languages amply suggests that the Austronesians were responsible for the development of Neolithic cultures in the North East India, the very first region through which it entered. Even the beliefs and practices of the present day tribal people of Arunachal have a similarity with that of the Burmese and other people of South East Asian countries in relation to these prehistoric tools. The tribes of Arunachal cherish Neoliths as charms and occasionally use them as amulets to ward off different kind of calamities and evils.

From the above discussion, it appears that Palaeolithic people had their habitation in this region. Like that the Neolithic culture in this religion does not seem to have an independent origin and typologically this culture comes closer to that of South East Asia. Ecological, linguistic and other historical evidences seem to indicate that this part was penetrated by prehistoric people from Yunan and Burma. It is noteworthy to mention here that the state still bears the cultural and economic pattern of the Neolithic people.

Excavation

Valuable knowledge is also unearthed because of the excavations of various sites in Arunachal Pradesh. The beginning in this regard was made in 1965-66 when L. N. Chakravarty carried out the first excavation in NEFA jointly with R. G. Pandey of the Archaeological Survey of India by which they were able to unearth a Siva Linga and remains of the Siva temple in the form of two bricks-built edifices datable to fourteenth-fifteenth century A.D. In 1966-67 Chakravarty again undertook excavations at Bhismaknagar in the Lohit district followed by Y. A. Raiker in 1968-70 which revealed a well- planned and well- protected city inhabited by people who reached a high degree of culture and civilisation. The materials unearthed show that apart from classical fort architecture, the people knew wheel-turned pottery terracotta art and advance metallurgy. The ruins datable to thirteenth -fourteenth century A.D. of the brick-built palace and the surrounding walls with massive gates and a ditch surrounding it, reflect the engineering skill of the people.

The Malinithan site in West Siang district, excavated by L. N. Chakravarty during 1970-72 unearthed the remains of a Brahminical temple, probably with subsidiary temples at different corners of the main temple dated about thirteenth - fourteenth century A.D. Beautiful icons of the Hindu deities discovered from this temple are variously datable to different periods between the tenth and fourteenth centuries A. D.[32] The Kalika Purana states that there was a Pithasthana east of Kamakhya and Malinithan is identified with that Pithasthana. Once a gigantic temple, it was built of stones as in other temples of India particularly those in Odisha of ninth to twelfth centuries A.D. The notable findings from Malinithan includes magnificent granite image of a bull, Ganapati, Surya, Kartikeya and Indra, besides some erotic sculptures.

The excavations carried out at Vijayanagar by Y. A. Raiker in the eastern part of the Tirap district in 1971 reveal a brick-built stupa with an external plaster in lime concrete. Among other noticeable finds as many as twenty-five small metal images of the Lord Buddha, and one clay figure of Buddha in *bhumisparsha mudra*, an octagonal silver Ahom coin and a few handmade potteries are noteworthy which are datable to eighteenth-nineteenth century A.D. He also undertook excavations at Rukmininagar in the Lower Dibang Valley during 1972-74 which unearthed light scattered brick ruins of a hill fort, remains of two brick rooms and the potteries identical with those found at Bhismaknagar. All such ruins confirm that a large fort existed at the place locally known as Rukmini Nati by the Idus (others call it Rukmininagar), datable to thirteenth -fourteenth century A.D. The Itafort at Itanagar excavated by Y.A Raiker during 1974-77 and later on by D. K. Bora of the State Research Department brought to light a fortified area enclosed by natural ridges and brick ramparts, the noteworthy being the findings of decorative bricks, a handful of coarse pottery, a metal representation of lion, carved stones in bas-relief, floral and animal designs, iron- clamps and nails.

The excavation at Naksaparvat in East Kameng district by D. K. Bora along with A. A. Ashraf of State Research Department during 1986- 90 was the first horizontal one. The site speaks of a single culture period having sixteen number of house plans mainly made of burnt bricks and mud mortars. The other remains include two ring wells, one made of finely chiselled dressed stone blocks of regular shapes and size and the other a typical one made of burnt clay, a large number of potteries, including glazed ware of Chinese celadon, handmade potteries, a dozen of carnelian beads, a new terracotta beads and the evidence of iron smelting kilns.

All such widely scattered archaeological remains at different places in Arunachal bear testimony to its rich cultural heritage. Excavations at Bhismaknagar in Dibang Valley which was once a stronghold of the Chutiyas of Assam between twelfth to sixteenth centuries A.D. reveal the high standard of civilisation that once prevailed in the state in ancient times.[33] Forts of Bhalukpong in the West Kameng district and of Itanagar so far yielding a few stone terracotta and metal figures, demonstrate various phases of cultural movements in Arunachal. Migration of different ethnic groups, their admixture and cultural contact with the world beyond its present geographical limits are vividly recorded amid the sculptural treasures as well as in other material remains.

Inscriptions

Inscriptions found within the boundaries of present day Arunachal so far known do not go beyond the fourteenth century A.D. Their short cryptic nature does not cite good details required for building up a satisfactory account of the territory based alone on their evidence. Still, the hidden truth of the epigraphic documents certainly renders them valuable as bedrocks of history of their respective periods offering definite information. Some of these bear specific dates while in case of others palaeography and circumstantial evidence help to ascertain their time and place of origin with a tolerant amount of certainty. Although the known specimens are very few in number, they offer some variety in language and script as well as in their subject matter. These are variously written in Assamese- Bengali, Tibetan, Newari, Tai and Burmese scripts. Even Sanskrit has been used on Assamese- Bengali characters.

The earliest inscription discovered in Arunachal is the Paya Tamresvari (Dikkaravasini) Temple. Inscription of *Muktadharmanarayana*, dated 1364, saka, i.e., 1442, A.D., noticed near Sadiya in the Lohit district. It is written in Sanskrit language and Assamese- Bengali script of the fifteenth century A.D. Again, the short legends inscribed on a number of bricks found from the Bhismakanagar Fort situated at a place not far removed from the Tamresvari Temple appear to contain a uniform formula repeating devotion to certain deities. These are not dated, but palaeographical consideration suggests some period between the fifteenth and sixteenth centuries A.D. The language and script used are Sanskrit and Assamese- Bengali respectively. All these throw some light on the political, religious and cultural history of the period.

Some other inscriptions need special mention here relevant to discussion held above. The Sadiya Pillar Inscription was situated in the vicinity of the old Sadiya town as established by the British on the way to Nizamghat. This serpent Pillar inscription records the terms of the treaty of the Ahoms with the Mishmis, executed in 1687 A.D. It is in Ahom language and refers to the confirmation of the Mishmis in their possession of the hills near Dibang river on payment of tribute and thus throws light on the political history of Arunachal Pradesh during the Ahom rule over Assam. Two inscribed guns of the time of the Ahom king Gadadhar Singha have been found from Chowkham in the Lohit district. They are in Assamese script and Sanskrit language bearing the date of Saka Era 1604, i.e., 1682 A.D.

Several tablets in the Buddhist monasteries, forts or dzongs, stupas or chortens and inscribed miniature chortens, stone plaques and pedestals of images are found in plenty among the habitats of the Vajrayana Buddhist population of Tawang, West Kameng and Upper Siang districts. These have not been properly studied. A memorial stone inscription is also found amid the ruins of Nakshaparvat in East Kameng district. These are written in Tibetan or Newari scripts and Sanskrit or Tibetan languages. All these taken together furnish information which help verify, corroborate and supplement evidence available from other sources.

Coins

Numismatic evidence is one of the most reliable sources for the study of early history of any land especially when the coins help us in determining the chronology of a dynasty. But unfortunately, not a single coin of Arunachal has been noticed, except the lone Ahom coin from Tirap district. An octagonal silver coin probably of Ahom king Gaurinath Singha (1780-1794) has been found at Vijayanagar Stupa area in Tirap. This shows that when the Ahom currency was in use, the Buddhist stupa site at Vijayanagar was a living centre.

B. Literary Sources

There is almost a complete absence of literary sources of history in the regional languages of Arunachal Pradesh. Since most of the tribes lack a script, they have not been able to preserve any recorded history, exceptions being the Khamptis of the Lohit district and the Monpas of the Kameng district. The Khamptis who came to Assam in the later part of the eighteenth century, possess a script derived originally from the Tai language. The Khampti literature mainly deals with Buddhist tenets, way of life, cosmology and mythology. There is one Khampti manuscript which contains a complete criminal code, enumerating punishments for both trivial and serious offences. The Khamptis also maintain some form of historical records called *Chyatuie*, which consists of writings on law, social and political events. But unfortunately, these sources more or less remain to be explored.

The Monpas of Kameng have been able to preserve many canonical literature of the Mahayana School of Buddhism like *Tanjur* and *Kanjur* in the Tibetan script in various ancient monasteries including the Great Tawang Monastery. The monasteries are also said to have preserved some records in the form of account books, agreements, sanads and parwanas. However, all these Khampti and Monpa regional literature provide useful references about the people, their contacts with Myanmar and China respectively and their religious activities.

The literary sources used for the historical reconstruction of the past of Arunachal Pradesh have been conveniently divided into (i) Brahminical Literature (ii) Accounts of Greek and Chinese Travellers (iii) Mohammedan Literature (iv) Buranjis and (v) British Literature. Let us have some discussion on them.

Brahminical Literature

Starting from the earliest phase of Indian literary history there are covert references to the non- Aryan autochthons like the *Nisadas, Kiratas* etc. and their settlements. Many of these accounts from the nature of their hints and description may be taken as related to the areas and people representing the present region designated as Arunachal Pradesh and its folk. The later Vedic and the early section of the Brahminical literature viz., the *Taittiriya Brahmana* and the *Vajasaneyi Samhita* of the *Yajurveda* as well as the *Atharvaveda* contain frequent mention of the hill people as well as herbs and plants growing in this country. The term *Kirata* occurs in the *Yajurveda* and *Atharvaveda,* the Ramayana and the Mahabharata; other ancient scriptures also refer to the Indo-Mongoloid people living in the hills and villages of the Himalayas and sub-Himalayan north-eastern hills of India.

The *Sabhaparva* of the Mahabharata states that Bhagadatta, the King of Pragjyotisa in Assam, with his *Cina* and *Kirata* soldiers took the side of the Kauravas in the battle of Mahabharata, the *Kiratas* and *Cinas* may be identified with the tribes of the adjacent hills. S. K. Chatterjee believes that the *Kiratas* of the Mahabharata were dwellers in the Himalayan region, particularly in the eastern Himalayas. According to Chatterjee, the north Assam tribes including the Adis of Arunachal may be reasonably identified with the *Kiratas.* This is how a relation is believed to have been established between the Vedic Aryans and the people of Arunachal Pradesh before the Christian era. Even the *Kalika Purana* and the *Yogini Tantra* also refer to *Kiratas*, to indicate the hill tribes of southern and eastern Himalayas. While the *Kalika Purana* describes Parasuram Kund (found in Lohit district of Arunachal) as a sacred place, the *Yogini Tantra* mentions about the washing away of sins with a bath in the same Kund. Besides reference to trans- Himalayan tracts continued to be there in the Puranas, the Buddhist and Hindu Tantric Literature like *Rudra Yamala, Vishnu Yamala, Kalika Purana and Yogini Tantra.*

Accounts of Greek and Chinese Travellers

Some works of both indigenous and foreign origin occasionally reveal awareness about Arunachal Pradesh. A few Greek travellers to India in early Christian era refer to the land and people of Arunachal. Pliny, in his book, *Natural History* written in first century A.D, gives us an indication that these people were the Tibeto-Burman tribes of Northern

Assam. Pliny refers to the people like *Syrites*, *Mandai*, *Ornulae*, *Coribae* and the *Abali*. Among them the *Ornulae* and *Abali* are identified as the Akas of present West Kameng district and the Abors (Adis) of East Siang district of Arunachal respectively. Ptolemy in the first half of the second century A.D. also refers to the various tribes of eastern India, many of them are of Bodo origin. Among his list can be noticed the tribes like *Amina khai*, identified as the Apatanis of Lower Subansiri district of Arunachal. He also refers the river *Sobanas* (presently Subansiri) and Dihong (Brahmaputra's indigenous name). Some of the hills mentioned by Ptolemy have been identified by Taylor as various hills of the present day Arunachal. Quite apropos to mention here that the *Annubi Hill* (identified with the Aka Hill) *Casius Hill* (perhaps the Mishmi hill), the *Mount Thagarus* (which appears to be the mount of Reging in the Adi area) and the chain of the *Emodi* (Himalayas), probably the mountain range separating Assam from Tibet.[34]

Even the Geography of Ptolemy (C.150 A.D.) states that *Serica*, a country probably located in Assam, is bounded in the east and the north by the hills and forests where canes are used for bridges. This refers probably to the remarkable cane bridges of the Adis of ancient Arunachal, who even today are famous for their beautiful artistic cane bridges. The term *Kirrhadae* is also mentioned in *Periplus of the Erythrean Sea* and Ptolemy's Geography indicating to the country of the Kiratas, extending from the far- off North- east India to south east Bengal. In seventh century A.D., Yuan Chwang, the Chinese traveller is said to have mentioned about the Adis of Arunachal, as mentioned by Edward Gait in his book *A History of Assam*.

Muhammedan Literature

The Muslim Chroniclers in the wake of Muslim invasion to Assam during the Ahom rule refer to the hill tracts of Arunachal. Muhammed Kasim, a Muslim historian, left an account of the Nyishis living independent of the Assam Raja and plundering the country contiguous to their mountains whenever finding opportunities. Shihabuddin Talish, the historian accompanying Mir Jumla, the Governor of Bengal during his expedition to Assam (1662-63), writes in his book Fathiyah-i-Ibriyah about the Mishmis and Miris and their trade relations with the plains of Assam. Talish writes, "It (Arunachal) is another world, another people with other customs. Its roads are frightful like the paths leading to the nook of death". Even he speaks about unpredictable seasons being experienced in Arunachal beginning at the time of their close elsewhere and the sky sending downpours without the clouds being shown.

Buranjis

The Ahom Buranjis (a class of documents of medieval Assam) which provide elaborate accounts of medieval Assam contain references to the people of Arunachal. The relation of the Arunachal tribes with Ahom monarchs has been recorded in details which are useful for conjuring up the political history of Arunachal. These Buranjis deal with the diplomatic correspondence, warfare, appointments and dismissal of ministers, officers etc. The Buranjis of the earlier period were written in Tai- Ahom language and from sixteenth century A.D. onwards they were written in Assamese. They provide us various trustworthy references about the hill tribes of the North-East Frontier on the basis of which history of Arunachal has been conceived possible. Various Buranjis refer to different aspects of socio, economic and cultural history of Arunachal.

Harkant Barua's *Assam Buranji* highlights about the Posa system of a kind of protective bribe being paid to the neighbouring tribes, like the Hill Miris, the Akas, the Adis and the Daflas (Nyishis) by the Ahom rulers to refrain them from frequent raids on the plains of Assam. Even Naobaicha Phukan's *Assam Buranji* refers to this system and indicates too how the Ahoms appointed a section of Miris as soldiers (good archers) in their army. Further, Kasinath Tamuli Phukan's *Assam Buranji* and Gunabhiram Barua's *Assam Baranjis* account for the Ahom- Miri relations. An idea of the

Ahom- Dafla (Nyishi) relations can be gleaned from *Deodhai Assam Buranji* and *Purani Assam Buranji* by Hema Chandra Goswami. Even the *Jayantia Buranji* gives an account of the participation of the Nyishis in the Jayantia expedition. The Ahom-Mishmi relations can be studied from the *Assam Buranji* of Harkant Barua, *Ahom Buranji* and *Purani Assam Buranji* of H. C. Goswami.

The *Ahom Buranji* and the *Tungkhungia Buranji* refer to the Khampti occupation of Sadiya and Khampti's fight against the Ahoms in 1799 A.D., supported by the Abors, Miris and Mishmis. The *Tungkhungia Buranji* and *Ahomar Sesh Yugar Buranji* mention about Ahom-Singpho relations. They also provide detailed description of the Moamaria Rebellion and the participation of the Nyishis and the Miris in this rebellion against the Ahom Government. They also provide us useful data regarding the Ahom- Bhutia relations. Besides these, the *Assam Buranji- A History of Assam from 1648 to1685*, edited by S.K. Dutta gives an important clue regarding the construction of Itafort (presently at Itanagar). All these go to suggest that the Buranjis play an important role in reconstructing the history of the medieval Arunachal.

British Literature

With the advent of the British a new trend was set in history writing. Most of the English writers were not professional historians, but basically administrators or military officers. Their knowledge of the North-East and its people proved milestone for compilation of a number of worthy historical works. The beginning was made by J. P. Wade accompanying Captain Welsh to Assam in 1792 as a doctor who compiled his translated version of Assamese Buranjis titled *An Account of Assam* together with a graphic geographical account captioned *A Geographical Sketch of Assam*.

Another very redeeming feature of ninetieth century historiography is the publication of scores of books and accounts on the frontier tribes. The students of tribal history today recall with gratitude the contributions made by some

European officers towards advancement of historical studies. Their intimate knowledge of the tribal customs and institutions and their exploratory habits always placed them on a more advantageous position than the native writers. The result was the production of some highly informative narratives on almost all the major tribes of North-East India.[35] Arunachal stood no exception to it. T. T. Cooper's *The Mishmi Hills* of 1873 and C. R. Macgregor's *Military Report on the Khamti - Singphoe Country* of 1887 bear the testimony to the statement made above.

The foundation of the Historical Institute '*The Asiatic Society of Bengal*' in 1784 by Sir William Jones and the '*Journals of the Asiatic Society of Bengal*' further promoted the research into topography, history and culture of the North-Eastern Hill Tribes. Apart from Official Records, the Reports on the military expeditions of the British officers against these tribes and the individual accounts kept by them on their publications formed the first stage in the direction of writing history and culture of the hill people of North-East India.

The earliest references on a tribe of Arunachal opening a window to colonial historiography can be traced back to 1791, i.e., on Daflas (presently known Nyishis) when the second volume of the *Asiatic Researches* of the Asiatic Society featured a translated article entitled *A Description of Assam* by Henry Vansittart.[36] Its 16th volume published in 1828, also included John Bryan Neufville's *Geography and Population of Assam*, an article referring the Abors (Adis), Miris and Mishmis as experts in bows and arrows containing poison on the tips. The 'Journal of the Asiatic Society of Bengal' published since 1840, through its several issues, made numerous mentions on the life and civilisation of the people of the North-East India.

A number of agreements executed by the British Raj with the chiefs and representatives of different tribal communities at different points of time, i.e., with the Singphos[37] (presently in Changlang and Lohit districts) in 1826; Khamptis[38] (Tirap) in 1843; Shertukpens[39] (West Kameng) in 1844; Akas[40] (West

Kameng) in 1844 and 1888 and the Adis[41] (East and West Siang) between 1862 to 1866, legitimising the former's political control over the latter prove today an asset of historiography. It is also attested by some of the primary source papers generated during the colonial rule.[42] "The Khamptis represent", as R. B. Pemberton writes, "the Shan culture of upper Burma. They migrated to their present place of Arunachal from their original home which was near the sources of the Irrawadi River. They follow the Buddhist religion".[43] According to W. Robinson, the Singphos who drove away the Khamptis from the lands below the Patkai Hills and settled themselves on the bank of the Tengapani River are most humorous tribes bordering on Assam valley.[44]

S. F. Hannay in 1847, puts the identity of the Singphos as a section of the Tesan group of the Burmese Kachin (Kachin and Shan or Kakhyen tribes of Burma are put into five groups- Tesan, Mirip, Lophae, Lotong and Myurung by Hannay)[45] who had migrated to Assam and occupied the western part of the Patkai Range.

We also find different historiographical narratives originating from the British administrator-scholars during the colonial period on a very important political issue, i.e., the 'Posa System' which stands still in vogue. Posa is defined officially as allowances paid to certain hill tribes inhabiting the hills on the northern frontier of Assam bordering Darrang and Lakhimpur, on account of commuted 'blackmail', or in consideration of the abandonment by them of their claims with regards to certain duars.[46] H. J. Peet, Deputy Commissioner of Lakhimpur, in his Letter No. 641G dated 05.8.1882 stated: "The word Posa literally means a collection of subscription for a common purpose- the word is well understood in this sense in Upper Assam".[47] Another scholar Mr W. Robinson, Inspector of Government Schools on Assam in his article also corroborates facts about Posa. He informs, "During the latter days of Ahom suzerainty when dissensions and the growing imbecility of the Government furnished opportunities for the bordering tribes to indulge in acts of rapine and lawless aggression on their low land neighbours, the Daphlas were not slow in exacting their share of the general spoil. Several attempts were made to check their atrocities and on one occasion the Ahom ruler Raja Gaurinath Singha, is said to have marched an army into their hills for the purpose of chastising them; when as native historians tell us, several thousand Daphlas were taken prisoners and brought down to the plains".[48]

In 1881 C. W. Beresford, writing about the Mishmi tribe living presently in the Lohit district of Arunachal claims, the Mishmis who lived to the west of the Digaru river were called as Digaru tribes by the British.[49] On the origin and writing of the past history of the Arunachali tribes, we gather some information from R.G. Woodthorpe's work whereby he goes to say that like the other tribes of the North East India the real origin of the tribes of Arunachal Pradesh is shrouded in mystery and doubt. The written history of these tribes before the arrival of the British to this part is not available. Probably due to illiteracy prevailed among these tribes, they could not write their past. They lived in such inhospitable mountainous terrains that the people from the plains could not establish any contact with them which resulted in the scant information on their early history and origin.[50] C. H. Lepper in 1882, mentions about the Singpho and Khampti tribes living independently in the Hukwang Valley before their migration to the North-Eastern part of India. But when they settled in the hilly areas of Assam, they accepted the sovereignty of the Assamese rulers.[51]

Woodthorpe's *General Report on the Topological Surveys of India for 1874-75,* also contains valuable references to the geography and people of the hills. Captain John F. Mitchell's *Report (Topographical, Political and Military) on the North East Frontier of India*, first published, Calcutta, 1883, under the title *The North East Frontier of India* contains reports on the Abors (Adis), Mishmis, Singphos, Khamptis, Miris and Daphlas (Nyishis) giving their geographical position and topographical history and a chronicle containing all the important events connected with each tribe for hundred years. It also showed their military operations and political relations with each of the tribes and the routes into their territories. Moreover, C. R. Macgregor's article '*Notes on Akas and Akaland*', published in the Proceedings of Asiatic Society of Bengal, Calcutta in 1884 proves to be a worthy treasure on the Akas living in the West Kameng District of Arunachal Pradesh.

J. F. Needham's '*Report on a trip into the Abor Hills, 1884*' (Shillong, 1885) and '*On the Bebejia Mishmi Expedition, 1889-1900*' (Shillong, 1900); G.W. Dun's '*Preliminary Notes on Daphlas*' (Simla, 1896) and *'Preliminary Notes on Miris'* (Simla, 1896) are the reports narrating the life style of the people which are considered no less significant historiographical documents for today's scholars.

Capt. W. B. Hore's Report on the Adi country regarding the outcome of the operations against the Adi villages responsible for the murder of Mr W. Williamson, the then Assistant Political Officer, Sadiya, Assam on 31st March, 1911, provides wholesome information. He writes, "The results of the operations were that punishment was inflicted on the hostile villages. All the men who had particularly participated in Mr Williamson's murder were caught, tried and sentenced and all rifles looted were restored. The country was traversed throughout its length and breadth

Several other reports of the British officers on their exploration missions into the then Arunachal and even ethnological reports throw light on the socio-politico-economic and environmental history of the tribes of Arunachal Pradesh. F. M. Bailey's '*Report on an Exploration on the North East Frontier, 1913*', (Simla, 1914); Major C. Bliss's '*Report on the Debong Survey and Exploration Mission*' (Shillong, 1914); Captain R.S. Kennedy's (Captain Kennedy was the Medical Officer of the Aka Promenade of 1913-14) '*Ethnological Report on the Akas, Khoas, Mijis and Membas of Tawang*' (Shillong, 1914) and G. Duff-Sutherland Dunbar's '*Abors and Galongs (Memoirs of Asiatic Society of Bengal, Vol.V, 1913-17)*' give several accounts of different tribes of the time of the state like

Mishmis, Khambas, Akas, Khowas (presently known as Buguns), Mijis and Monpas. Maxwell, the Political Officer also reports on the nature of the Akas. He goes to say that if all the savage races of the North-Frontier of Assam Province were compared, the Akas had been meant more contumacious and troublesome[53] who used to commit raids on the plains people of Assam for collection of 'Posa' by force and to plunder them.

The multiplicity of tribes in Arunachal (the major tribes being noted in 1945[54] were Bhutia, Daphla, Miri, Adi, Mishmi, Khampti, Singpho, Nishi, Tagin, Apatani, Wancho etc.) and their heterogeneity are due to the confinement to their respective ridges and mountainous terrains after migrating to this part in different groups.[55] Because of their long isolationistic character, all of them developed their separate and independent way of living. When they came in contact with the British by ninetieth century, the Western Missionaries influenced several tribes of the areas resulting in the Christianity appearing as a great religious force not only in Arunachal Pradesh but also all over the hilly areas of Assam which largely changed the social and cultural outlook of the hill people. This is what Mr W.C. Smith reports in 1923.[56] These are not less historiographical testimony to encourage the scholars to delve deep into them for writing history on the state.

Moreover, R. C. Cunning's notes on the Abors and Miris[57]; H. I. Halliday's '*The Abors of Assam*', *United Empire,* Vol. XIX (1928); J. F. Needham's 'Report on the Abor villages beyond the British Frontier (1884)' *Assam Review*, Vol. II, No.7 (1929); P. G. Huddleston's '*Abor Military and Political Mission 1912-15*', *R. Engineering Journal*, Vol. XLIV (1930); N. L. Bor's '*The Daphlas and their Oaths*', *JRASB*, Vol. II (Third Series, 1936); N. L. Bor's '*A Sketch of the Vegetation of the Aka Hills, Assam: A Synecological Study*', *Indian Forest Records, N.S. Botany*, Vol. I (1938); C. von Furer- Haimendorf's '*Agriculture and Land Tenure among the Apa Tanis*', *Man in India*, Vol. XXVI (1946); C. von and E. von Furer- Haimendorf's

'*Notes on Tribal Justice among the Apa Tanis*', *Man in India*, Vol. XXVI (1946) and J. P. Mills' '*A Brief Note on Agriculture in the Dirang Dzong Area*', *Man in India*, Vol. XXVI (1946) too speak high of historiographical sources to excavate archaeology of information on the different tribes of the state like the Abors, Nyishis, Akas, Apatanis and Monpas.

Large number of documents written and compiled by the British Officers in the colonial period, both civil and military, on their interaction with the various tribes of Arunachal stand milestone as historiographical compendium projecting the geographical, climatic and the laws and customs of the people. The publication of monographs on various hill tribes of North east India is one of the most outstanding contributions of the British towards the understanding of the tribes of the hills. With the gradual extension of their power over these hills, the British came in more contact with these diverse hill people and felt it necessary to know more about them for effective administration.

The first and the most productive work on the history and commerce of Assam with references to commercial products of the then Arunachal getting exchanged in the plains of Assam, was undertaken by Captain Welsh's collaborator, Dr John Peter Wade who compiled *An Account of Assam* during 1794-1800 from indigenous sources and deposited it in the India Office Library, London, which was edited and published by Benudhar Sharma in 1927. One more work of Dr Wade was *Geographical Sketch of Assam*, compiled during 1786-1802, edited and published by S. K. Bhuyan as discourse-series in the *Assam Review*, Silchar in 1928-29 under the title '*Assam in the Eighteenth Century*' deals with the information on the division of rivers, towns, villages and productions of the province in which references were made to the surrounding hills, people and their products. *The Frontier* (London, 1832) by G. Dunbar refers to the geography and the people of the hills on North-East India. John M'Cosh's *Topography of Assam* (London, 1837) also acknowledges information on the extent of territories, cultivations, governments, houses, migration, trade and customs of the tribes of Arunachal like the Daphlas (Nyishis), Kapachors (one group of the Akas), Miris, Abors (Adis), Mishmis, Kamtis (Khamptis) and Singphos.[58]

A Descriptive Account of Assam (Calcutta, 1841) by William Robinson who got associated with the education of Assam for a long period and the first Inspector of Schools, Brahmaputra Valley, puts a vivid account on the extent of territories, habits, manners, customs of the hill tribes, such as the Akas, Daphlas, Miris, Abors, Mishmis, Khamtis and Singphos of Arunachal. John Butler's *A Sketch of Assam with some Accounts of the Hill Tribes* (London, 1847) gives a picture of the early life of the hill people. While J. Beams in 1867 speaks about the Abor (Adi), Miri and Dafla (Nyishi) numerals[59], E.T. Dalton in 1872, gives accounts of the Khamptis, Singphos, Mishmis, Abors (Adis), Daflas (Nyishi) and Akas.[60] T. T. Cooper's *The Mishmee Hills* (London, 1873) deals with his visits to the Mishmi areas and his encounters with them. *A Statistical Account of Assam,* Vols. II and III (London, 1879) of W. W. Hunter is another important source book for the study of the hill people of the region. Moreover, G. Campbell[61] also describes about Adis and Nyishis and gives their vocabularies in 1874.

The most outstanding historical work *History of the Relations of the Government with the Hill Tribes of North-East Frontier of Bengal* (Calcutta, 1884) of Alexander Mackenzie based on a detailed examination of all the records from 1780 till 1882 from the Bengal Secretariat and Foreign Department and the Assam Annual Administrative Reports deals not only the political history of the North-East Frontier but also its people's manners, customs and ethnological affinities. Mackenzie's theory of migration of the Singphos[62]; J. F. Needham's monographs[63] on Singpho and Khampti languages and on the Abor Hills; J. D. Anderson's *Short Vocabulary of the Aka Language* (Shillong, 1896); W. Crooke's *Abor, Abor-Miri, Hasting's Encyclopaedia of Religion and Ethics* (London, 1908), Vol. I; G. A. Grierson's *Linguistic Survey of*

India, Vol. III, *Tibeto-Burman Family*, Pt. I (Calcutta, 1909) and J. H. Lorrain's *A Dictionary of the Abor-Miri Language with Illustrative Sentences and Notes* (Shillong, 1910) go to give us a lot of historical sources on the languages, religion and ethics of different tribes of Arunachal like the Singphos, Khamptis, Adis, Akas, Miris, Nyishis and Mishmis.

The historical work *A History of Assam* (London, 1905) by Sir Edward Gait, the magnum opus, has been acclaimed as the most valuable work on the history of North-East India by all students and researchers, a classic of its kind. B. C. Allen's multivolume, *Assam Gazetteer* (Calcutta, 1906) is a basic work for the study on the history of the people of North-East India. His other work *The Imperial Gazetteer* (London, 1909) is a shorter account of the places and their people and is an invaluable work on the history of this area.

Even some of the works based on expedition- experiences prove to be worthy primary sources to decipher important information about the tribes during the period. Researchers are immensely benefited by such works to reach out closest to the facts available in the then period for placing them on records further with different research orientation and interpretation required in today's world. That is how Arunachal is still considered as the treasure-house of knowledge. Its unique social, religious, cultural, lingual and ethnic dialectics with tribal heterogeneity have attracted many a scholars to delve themselves deep into such ever-exploring social phenomena.

A. Hamilton's *In Abor Jungles* (London, 1912) which describes the Abor Expedition and the Mishmi and Miri Missions; P. Willington's *On the track of the Abor* (London, 1912); F. Kingdon- Ward's *A Plant Hunter in Tibet* (London, 1934) with two chapters detailed on the Mishmis; G. Dunbar's personal visit account on the environmental history being much sought after an inter-disciplinary issue of research in social science in the recent days of the state, calling the then flourishing villages of Arunachal within a valley midway between the foot-hills and the main snowy range, as the heart of the tribal country remaining insular from the influence of Assam with its Indian and western form of civilisation and it is too far for south to be affected by the religious ideas and customs of Tibet[64] and Kingdon-Ward's *Assam Adventure* (London, 1941) with references made to Monpas living in the western side of the state are worth-research published works to deal with Frontier History.

A Collection of Treaties, Engagements and Sanads, Vol. XIII (Calcutta, 1931) by C. U. Aitchison holds to be a very important document for the study of the British expansion in North-East India. One more work entitled *The Linguistic Survey of India* with its volumes II and III (Calcutta, 1909 and 1928) by Sir A. Grierson stands as a unique historical document containing an account on the hill tribes of North- East India. It deals with the division and classification of the people of India on the basis of linguistic similarities. Besides, it also provides an account of the tradition of their origin, migration and settlement on the basis of their linguistic affinities and oral traditions. The other commendable historical work that needs a special mention here is *History of the Frontier Areas Bordering on Assam, 1883-1941* (London, 1942) by Sir Robert Reid, taken to be a continuation one of A. Mackenzie's monograph of 1884 unto 1941. This way, Reid's work completes the history of British relations with the hill tribes of North-East India from their very first contact with the British till almost towards the fag end of the British hegemony in India.

Apart from the above literature various unpublished works like Political Proceedings, Secret Proceedings, Official Correspondences and Revenue Proceedings, Census Reports, Military Reports of the British period serve as primary source for the study of the history of Arunachal. These various unpublished documents can be studied in the National Archives, New Delhi; the Asiatic Society of Bengal, Kolkata; the National Library, Kolkata and the Assam Secretariat Record Office, Guwahati etc. All these documents along with the various published monographs mentioned above give us almost an overall scenario of the social, political, economic and cultural history of the state.

Arunachal Pradesh (earlier NEFA), though treated as a land of insularity, had invited the attention of the British since the beginning of the British rule in India. Reports on the tribes of the state were prepared even before the annexation of Assam to the Company's territories. Great task was endorsed by the Company to Francis Hamilton (later known as Buchanon Hamilton) and R. B. Pemberton to prepare reports on the provinces on the Frontiers of Bengal. After Assam being annexed, the British officers, civil and military, posted in Assam were asked to prepare reports on the frontier tribes and the officers recorded their exploratory reports which though biased and fell short of introspection, stand cynosure for providing valuable information on the different aspects of tribal life in the state of the time.

Though the colonial rule never attempted to prepare a synchronised account of the different tribes of the Frontier region, efforts were made from 1881 onwards to include monographs on the Frontier tribes in the Census of India Reports. Thus, by 1947 all but the tribes of the western hills and those who lived on the fringes of the border were covered in these reports. But such reports were found suffering from inaccuracy, particularly in respect of statistical data, as the officers rarely went inside the hills to collect them. But monographs and different accounts on different tribes although biased began to appear. "Such bewildering mass of reports and accounts of various kinds are elusive, some are biased, others suffer from lack of understanding and a few are partial and incomplete".[65] Despite criticisms being labelled against such works published and documented during colonial period by the British officials on Arunachal Pradesh, they are considered as the basic and solid sources of historiography for carrying out interdisciplinary research on the heterogeneous tribal societies in all their aspects of the contemporary period and beyond, with exceptions of skeptic misunderstanding on the varied nature of the tribes, sub-tribes, clan structure and names of the places.

References

1. R.C. Woodthorpe, "Notes on the Wild Tribes inhabiting the so-called Naga Hills of North-East Frontier of India", *Journal of Royal Anthropological Institute*, Vol. II, Calcutta, 1882, pp. 56-72.
2. S.K. Chatterjee, "Kirata- Jana Krit", *Journal of Royal Asiatic Society of Bengal,* Vol. XVI, Calcutta, 1950, p.145.
3. S.K. Chatterjee, "Kirata- Jana Krit, Indo- Mongoloids: Their Contribution to the History and Culture of India", *Journal of Royal Asiatic Society of Bengal,* Vol. XVI, No. 2, Calcutta, 1950, p. 22.
4. J.C. White, *Sikkim and Bhutan*, Delhi, 1971, pp. 7-10.
5. W.C. Smith, *The Naga Tribes of Assam,* London, 1825, pp.153-160.
6. S.K. Chatterjee, "Kirata- Jana Krit", *Journal of Royal Asiatic Society of Bengal, op. cit.*, p.145.
7. Chandrika Singh, *Political Evolution of Nagaland*, New Delhi, 1981, pp.6-7.
8. *Ibid*, *Emergence of Arunachal Pradesh as a State*, Delhi, 1989, p.20.
9. *Ibid*, pp. 20- 21.
10. A.C. Talukdar, "Political Evolution of Arunachal Pradesh", *Proceedings of North-East India History Association* (hence PNEIHA), Pasighat, 1986, p.131.
11. K.S. Singh (Ed), *People of India- Arunachal Pradesh*, Vol.XIV, Calcutta, 1995, p.35.
12. M.L. Bose, *British Policy in the North-East Frontier Agency*, New Delhi, 1979, p. 93.
13. K.S. Singh (ed), *op.cit*, p.10.
14. *Ibid*, p. 216.
15. *Ibid*, p.288.
16. D. Pandey and B.K. Tripathy, *A Comprehensive History of Arunachal Pradesh*, Pasighat, 1997, p. 73.
17. D.K. Palit, *Sentinels of the North-East: The Assam Rifles*, New Delhi, 1984, p. 21.
18. A. Hamilton, *In Abor Jungles of North-East India*, Delhi, 1984 (Reprint), p.119.
19. Gurudas Das, "In Corporation of Arunachal Hills into Colonial British India: A Politico- Economic Analysis", *PNEIHA*, Doimukh, 1994, P.335.
20. Alastair Lamb, *Britain and Chinese Central Asia*, London, 1960, p. 337.
21. L.N. Chakravarty, *Glimpses of the Early History of Arunachal*, Directorate Research, Government of Arunachal Pradesh, Itanagar, 1995, p. 6.

22. *Ibid*, p. 12.
23. A. Mackenzie, *History of the Relations of the Government with the Hill Tribes of the North- East Frontier of Bengal*, Calcutta, 1884, p.16.
24. L.N. Chakravarty, *op.cit,* pp.37-38.
25. *Ibid*, p.85.
26. *Ibid*, p.78.
27. J.N. Chowdhury, *Arunachal Through the Ages*, Shillong, 1982, pp.154-9.
28. L.N. Chakravarty, *op.cit,* p.79.
29. *Ibid*, p. 8.
30. D. Pandey and B.K. Tripathy, *op.cit,* pp. 13-14.
31. *Ibid*, pp.14- 15.
32. Subid Chatterjee, *op.cit,* pp. 6-7.
33. A.K. Thakur, "Archaeologoy of Arunachal Pradesh", *ICHR Project Report*, New Delhi, 2004.
34. D. Pandey and B.K. Tripathy, *op.cit,* pp. 6-7.
35. S.D. Goswami, "Progress of Historical Research in North-East India: A Survey", (*PNEIHA*), 14th Session, Jorhat, 1993, p. 357.
36. M. S. Sangma, "Presidential Address", *PNEIHA*, 15th Session, Doimukh, 1994, p. 3.
37. C. U. Aitchison, *A Collection of Treaties, Engagements and Sanads,* Vol. XII, 1973 (Reprint), Government of India Central Publication Branch, pp. 119-120 and pp. 142-143.
38. *Ibid*, p. 148.
39. *Ibid*, pp. 150-151.
40. *Ibid*, pp. 164-165.
41. *Ibid*, pp. 156-162.
42. See Selection of Papers; Regarding the Hill Tracts between Assam and Burma and on the Upper Brahmaputra, 1825-70, Calcutta, 1873.
43. R. B. Pemberton, *Report on the Eastern Frontier of the British India,* Calcutta, 1835, p. 70.
44. W. Robinson, *A Descriptive Account of Assam*, London, 1841, p. 373.
45. S. F. Hannay, *Sketch of the Singphos or the Kakhyens of Burma*, Calcutta, 1847, Tract 266, p. 7.
46. L.N. Chakravarty, *op. cit.,* p. 122.
47. *Ibid.*
48. W. Robinson, "Notes on the Daphlas and the Peculiarities of their Language", *Journal of the Asiatic Society of Bengal* (*JASB*), No. 2, 1851, pp. 126-127.

49. C. W. Beresford, *Notes on the North-East Frontier of Assam*, Shillong, 1881, p. 28; Also see, Chandrika Singh, *op. cit.*, p.12.
50. R. G. Woodthorpe, "Notes on the Wild Tribes inhabiting the so- called Naga Hills on North- East Frontier of India", *Journal of Royal Anthropological Institute,* Vol. II, Calcutta, 1882, pp. 56-72 and pp. 196-212.
51. C. H. Lepper, "Notes on the Singpho and Khampti Country of North East Frontier", *Proceedings of Asiatic Society of Bengal*, Calcutta, 1882.
52. Capt. W. B. Hore, *Report on the Abor Country*, Simla, 1913, p. 10.
53. Report of Maxwell, Foreign Department, Ext. A, Progg., October 18, 1914, Nos. 41-116.
54. See *North and North-East Frontier Tribes of India*, compiled in Intelligence Branch Division of the Chief of the British Army Staff, New Delhi, 1945, pp. 162-63.
55. S. Barkataki, *Tribes of Assam*, Shillong, 1968, pp. 1-5; Also see, Chandrika Singh, *op. cit.*, p. 6.
56. W. C. Smith, "Missionary Activities and the Acculturation of Backward People", *Journal of Applied Sociology,* Vol. 7, Calcutta, 1923, pp. 15-18.
57. R. C. R. Cunning, "Notes on Certain Frontier Tribes", *Census of India, 1921*, Shillong, 1923, Vol. III, Assam, Pt. 1, Report, App. B, pp. 13-14.
58. M. S. Sangma, *op. cit.*, p. 7.
59. J. Beams, *Outline of Indian Philology*, Calcutta, 1867, Appendix.
60. E.T. Dalton, *Descriptive Ethnology of Bengal*, Calcutta, 1872; German Edition: Berlin, 1875, pp.1-38.
61. G. Campbell, *Specimens of the Languages of India, including those of the Aboriginal Tribes of Bengal, the Central Provinces and the Eastern Frontier*, Calcutta, 1874, pp. 21-35.
62. A. Mackenzie, *A History of the Government with the Hill Tribe of the North-East of Bengal*, Calcutta, 1884; Also see, C. H. Lepper, op. cit.; *Assam Buranji: A Chronicle of the Ahom Rule in Assam (1228-1826)*, by K. T. Phukan, Sibsagar, 1848 and L. W. Shakespeare, *History of Upper Assam, Upper Burma and North-East Frontier*, London, 1914.
63. J. F. Needham, *Outline Grammar of the Singpho Language*, Shillong, 1889; *Outline Grammar of the Khampti Language*, Shillong, 1894 and *Report of a Trip into the Abor Hills, 1884,* Shillong, 1895.
64. G. Dunbar, *Other Men's Lives*, London, 1938, pp. 230-31.
65. M. L. Bose, *op. cit.,* Preface, p. vii.

Chapter - 3

Periodisation vis-à-vis History of Arunachal Pradesh

Periodisation of the history of Arunachal Pradesh on the basis of the historical sources available, considered so far being very scanty and inadequate, in the line of the conventional pattern of Ancient, Medieval and Modern as the history of a particular state of our country goes, is not so easy a profession. Acute dearth of sources renders scholars strains putting the phases of history of Arunachal into the parameter of justification of phases of Indian History. The discussion on this aspect is detailed out in the next chapter. Still, for the sake of convenience of the readers reconstruction of history of Arunachal into Ancient, Medieval and Modern has been suitably made by the scholars, not in congruence with the parameter of division of Indian history. Let us throw some light on them to hold our discussion relevant in the next chapter.

Ancient Period

The state being the trans- Himalaya hilly region bordering Tibet and China in the north Pragjyotishpur or Kamrupa (Assam) in the south, Burma (Myanmar) in the east and Bhutan in the west, remained an unknown and insular one. P.C. Choudhury goes to say that ancient Kamrupa included Bhutan, Tibet, hilly areas of Assam, some portion of Bengal,

Tripura and Myemensingh (presently in Bangladesh) etc. Arunachal Pradesh, as he suggests, was a part of ancient Kamrupa. However, Arunachal did not get included in the ancient Kamrupa which seems evident from the existence of independent and powerful kingdoms of Bidarbha (Lower Dibang Valley), Chedi (Tezu areas of Lohit Valley), Kalita (Anjaw Valley) and Bhalukpong (Lower Kameng Valley) of Arunachal Pradesh. Even the *Yogini Tantra* also excludes Arunachal from the ancient kingdom of Kamrupa which goes to mention that Kamrupa included the whole of Brahmaputra valley, Bhutan, Rangpur district of Bangladesh, Cooch Behar and probably the Garo Hills of Meghalaya.

It is therefore believed that the ancient Arunachal Pradesh was probably either an ally of Kamrupa or it acknowledged the suzerainty of the ancient Kamrupa. It is also evident from the fact that the hill tribes of Arunachal Pradesh known as the *Kiratas* and *Cinas* helped Bhagadatta, the king of Kamrupa in his war against the Pandavas. It is said that the Kaurava prince, Duryodhana married Bhanumati, the daughter of Bhagadatta and the king Bhagadatta along with the *Kirata and Cina* soldiers fought in the Mahabharata war against the Pandavas. Hence, the territory of ancient Arunachal Pradesh apparently extended upto the Myang province and Pemako valley (Kham province of Tibet in the north, the Brahmaputra River in the south, Myanmar in the east and 6 in the west).

Mystery so far has not been unearthed to determine the history of the ancient Arunachal. Limited sources throw very grey ray on its history. Caves and stones bearing foot marks of man, animal and bird, stone axes and other artifacts found in the state render some historical significance for study. Cave at Menga in Upper Subansiri district, similar caves at Padu village called *Sukreng- Bireng* and Damroh village areas in the Upper Siang district, footprint on a stone called *Peyang Lelam* and vagina on stone called *Mime Itti* at Padu village and footmarks of man, animal and bird on a stone called *Lui Batum* at Tigra village in East Siang district certainly speak of some historical ethics.[1] Even the recent excavation of stone axes and other artifacts from Komkar village in Upper Siang district by the Directorate of Research, Government of Arunachal Pradesh suggests some link of Arunachal with the Neolithic Age of the human race. The *Shiva Lingas* deciphered at various places in the jungles of Arunachal speak of its leverage to the cult of Lord Shiva. The historical ruins excavated at Bhalukpong in West Kameng district, Itanagar in Papum Pare district, Malinithan in West Siang district, Gomsi (Rani) in East Siang district and Bhismaknagar in Lower Dibang Valley district of Arunachal Pradesh suggest the state with some historical bearings in the ancient past.

The Epics like the *Ramayana* and *Mahabharata* throw some light on the material condition of the ancient Arunachal Pradesh. The *Ramayana* describes the people of this state as *Kiratas* clad in animal skins wearing thick top-knots called *Podum* and living on fruits and roots, probably the sweet potatoes. The *Mahabharata* describes the tribal people of Arunachal Pradesh as the *Kiratas* and *Chins* and extols their heroic and daring exploits in the Mahabharata War. The term *Kirata* is in fact a generic one applied to the tribes of whole North-East India with Mongoloid origin. The *Kalika Purana* refers to the present Subansiri Valley as *Prabhu Mountain* (on which once upon a time Hiranyakashyap ruled as the king with his son Prahallad as the legendary figure) and Upper Lohit Valley (now Anjaw district) as *Prabhu Kuthar* (on which once the king Daksha ruled with his beautiful daughter, Parvati getting married to Lord Shiva). Even the legend of Rukmini Haran tells us about *Bidarbha (* Lower Dibang Valley) on which once Bhismak was the king with his capital at Kundina, now being referred to Bhismaknagar, 26 kilometres from Roing town; about Chedi (Lower Lohit Valley) adjacent to the Kingdom of Bidarbha where once the King Sishupal (enemy of Lord Krishna of Dwarka) ruled and his descendants now being referred to the Digaru-Mishmis and also tells us about the marriage of Rukmini, the princess of Bidarbha with Krishna of Dwarka.

The *Bhagavat* and *Vishnu Purana* tell us about Bali, the King of Sonitpur, the city of blood (modern Tezpur) who had numerous sons, Bana being the eldest. He had to succeed his father after his death as the King of Sonitpur. Bana Raja, who happens to be the contemporary of Narakasur, the King of Kamrup had many sons and a beautiful daughter named Usha. The legend of *Kumar Haran* describes that Usha once dreamt of Aniruddha, the grandson of Lord Krishna and accepted him as her husband. She was able to kidnap Aniruddha with the help of her friend, Chitralekha who entered the heavily guarded castle where Usha was confined by her father and marriage between the two could be solemnised according to the *Gandharva* ceremony. Aniruddha was captured and rescued by Lord Krishna after defeating Bana Raja in a battle fought at a place, now being referred as Tezpur Bil. Bhaluk, the grandson of Bana Raja, the King of Sonitpur established a Kingdom at the foot of the Aka hills and made his capital at Bhalukpong. The ruins of old fortifications accredited to Bhaluk are still noticeable at Bhalukpong in the West Kameng district of Arunachal Pradesh, around 65 kilometres away from Tezpur, Assam. The Akas, earlier called Hrussos, proudly ascribe Bhaluk as their ancestor.

It is too pertinent here to discuss some other glories of ancient Arunachal Pradesh with their historicity and historical relevance, so far deciphered. Malinithan stands out to be a unique one. A place of great sanctity, it is situated in the lower region of West Siang district and associated with the God Shiva and Goddess Parvati. The *Kalika Purana* tells as that when Lord Krishna married Rukmini, the princess of Bidarbha (Lower Dibang Valley) and was on his way back to Dwarka (Gujarat), he rested at Malinithan where both of them were received by Lord Shiva and his consort, Parvati. Lord Krishna on welcome was offered a garland of the choicest flowers by Parvati for which she was addressed *Malini*, the mistress of choicest flowers and hence the place could be known as Malinithan. Here at, a temple complex is believed to have existed which enshrined various deities of whom the stone images of Goddess Durga, Lord Ganesh, a statue resembling Goddess Saraswati with violin, a magnificent bull- Nandi, the vehicle of Lord Shiva and Kartikeya are worth mentioning.

The approximate date of ruins of this temple has been placed as of the thirteenth and fourtenth century A.D.

One more kingdom, known to be highly civilised, named Kalita Kingdom is said to have been there at the vicinity of Rima in Upper Lohit Valley (now Anjaw district of Arunachal Pradesh). The tradition tells us that once Parsurama's father was humiliated by Parikshit, a Kshatriya King and hence Parsurama swore to exterminate the Kshatriya race from the surface of the earth. In order to save themselves from persecution and extirpation of Parsurama some kshatriyas fled to the far north east and established a Kalita kingdom in due course.

Another site excavated by the Department of Research, Government of Arunachal Pradesh, of bricks of ruined buildings at Gomsi (Rani Village) in East Siang district tells us about the existence of a prosperous capital city of a Hindu King. The local version depicts the existence of such a city to the west of Nari, a sub-divisional headquarters in East Siang district. The territory of that Hindu Kingdom apparently extended up to the Siang River to the east, probably the reason being, that king is said to have kept his second wife, Rani (queen) at Rani (Rani village) which is presently fifteen kilometres away from Pasighat, the district headquarters of East Siang. The local people believe that the capital city of that Hindu king got perished in one night due to the occurrence of a devastating flash flood. The entire population also got washed away with only one woman survivor to tell the tale of that shocking incident.

The legend further ascribes that the only woman survivor went eastwards and settled at Nari. She saw once some Adis in war dresses and anticipating herself to be killed by them, she asked them not to kill her in her own language *Abala narik namarib* (do not kill a helpless woman). She started repeating the same words again and again. The Adis hardly could understand her words and thought the woman being old and lonely probably wanted to die and was asking them to kill her. They therefore, killed her and the place where that lonely lady was killed came to be known as Nari after "*Nari*" uttered by that woman. Hence, the present village goes by the name *Rani* after Rani (queen) of that ill-fated king. As such we may ascribe the ruins of buildings at Gomsi (Rani) to the Baro-Bhuyans (twelve chiefs) who were feudatory kings of Kamata (Cooch Behar) kingdom and ruling the country north bank of the river Brahmaputra at that time. Since the Chutia Kingdom extended from the Brahmaputra in the east to the Subansiri River in the west on the north bank of Brahmaputra at the time of annexation of Chutia kingdom by the Ahom king Suhungmung in 1520, A.D, a Chutia ruler is believed to have been the founder of Gomsi (Rani Village).

The Epic *Mahabharata* describes Bhagadatta, the king of Kamrupa (Assam) as a powerful king ruling in the eastern India. It is said that once the Pandava prince Arjuna went out on a conquering campaign to the different parts of India. In course of his campaign he arrived in Pragjyotishpur (Kamrupa) and attacked the kingdom of Bhagadatta who with his large army of *Kirata* and *Chin* soldiers fought bravely with him but got defeated continuing the fight for eight days. The same epic also entails that the Kaurava and Pandava princes quarrelled for empire of India and they met in the battlefield of Kurukshetra (New Delhi), better known as the Mahabharata War (taking place in 1424, B.C. as suggested by famous historian Alexander Cunningham), for their final struggle. Bhagadatta, father-in-law of the Kaurava prince, Duryodhan, joined the war with his band of *Kirata* and *Chin* soldiers against the Pandava princes. But he succumbed to death against his combat with Arjuna. The Mahabharata is full of praises on the heroic and daring deeds of the *Kirata* and *Chin* soldiers of Bhagadatta's army. It says, "The Kiratas, with hair done in pointed top-knot, pleasant to look upon, shining like gold, able to move under water; are terrible and veritable tiger men so are they found."[2]

The term *Kirata* is a generic one used for the inhabitants of the trans-Himalayan mountain ranges (North-East India). *Chin* is the term used for the allies or kinsmen of *Kiratas* who were of Mongoloid origin. The Adis of East Siang and Upper Siang districts of Arunachal Pradesh display the closest resemblance to the Chins. The *Kirata* mentioned in the Mahabharata are the tribal people of Arunachal Pradesh and of North-East India. The Apatanis and Nyishis of the state still adore the same kind of hair styles as mentioned in the Epic till today.

Hence, it is believed as per the ruins of buildings excavated and legends prevalent, that ancient Arunachal Pradesh had almost eight kingdoms namely Prabhu Mountain, Prabhu Kuthara, Bidarbha, Chedi, Bhalukpong, Malinithan, Kalita and Gomsi (Rani) on which little discussion is held above. But no definite length of period has yet been ascertained as to when all these ancient kingdoms flourished and decayed. As discussed in the beginning dearth of historical records has rendered the ancient history of the state obscure. The Puranic literature, legends, myths and local says have pushed such history to an extent which it is presently found to be. Logical exposition of truth is traced out on the basis of the little historical and archaeological materials deciphered so far. But it does not fit into the logical and inquisitive minds of scholars of history. The issue of the royal dialectics under the purview of a historical diaspora in the form of king- kingdom relationship has been found to be a great missing link to make the history as found more sound and logistic as compared to history of the time in respect of other states in India. There is not an ounce of negativism displayed so far from any quarter to render such history more dynamism. But topographical bottlenecks, communicational handicaps and situational restrictions have worked hand in hand from time to time to place such history in a shape we are to be satisfied with, before the readers and scholars.

Medieval Period

The earliest epoch of human civilisation in Arunachal Pradesh as elsewhere in the Indian subcontinent is but vaguely known. But certain significant findings made so far have revealed some aspects of the peculiar pattern of development in this regard. Geologically, the mountains of Arunachal are of much later origin than the peninsular India which originally belonged to the continent known as Gondowana. The Himalayas, on the eastern fringes of which Arunachal is situated were formed gradually due to the rise of the bed of the ocean known as Tethys. Free movement of species in this ocean is evident from the similarity of fossil remains between different countries like Burma (Myanmar), China and North India including Arunachal. The close ethnic, linguistic and cultural affinity of the present tribes of the state with the different peoples of the neighbouring countries of South and South-East Asia are generally taken to indicate a common Mongoloid origin in distant past.

The original inhabitants of Arunachal Pradesh and north-eastern region may well be held associated as in the case of other parts of India, with the Old Stone Age and Microlithic cultures, evidences of which are gradually being revealed through recent researches in this area. Regarding the neoliths of the region including Arunachal a period around the first millennium B.C. has been suggested for their introduction on the basis of their correction with the Chinese neoliths and those of Burma and other South-East Asian countries, although possibility of a much earlier beginning in some more remote past cannot be precluded altogether. The arguments advanced by various scholars bringing down this date line have little real basis to be accepted as final. However, this culture along with the practice of raising the megaliths or big memorial stones and tombs, as are noticed in Meghalaya and also in the Kameng and Subansiri regions of Arunachal might have continued till very recent times.

As discussed above, the similarity of remains suggests affinity and similar development of human civilisation in the north eastern part of India and adjoining regions of South and South East Asia. Various movements in all these countries naturally affected present Arunachal Pradesh and vice versa. Penetration of different waves of the Sino- Tibetan speakers in the region falls in the same line. They appear to have entered India in course of their southern and westward movement from China since prehistoric times. Their large scale immigration, however, took place possibly around the first millennium B.C. All the dialects of the present tribal people of Arunachal broadly belong to this speech family- the Tibeto-Burman branch of the parent stock except those of the language of the Tai Khamptis, who entered the territory very late, being the Siamese- Chinese branch.

The waves of early Sino-Tibetan speakers could have entered both through the north western corridors and the north- eastern parts of the country across the Nepali, Bhutanese, Tibetan and Burmese frontiers, hill tracts of which have served as communication routes, though in limited scale, even in recent times and till now are being used as such by local tribal population. In the absence of other definite evidence, linguistic and ethnic materials available have been taken together to suppose that a number of these primitive people most probably entered these territories in pre- historic times from across the Tibetan borders. In the process the river course of the Tsangpo which is known as Siang in Arunachal Pradesh and ultimately as Brahmaputra in Assam, may have played an important role. Courses of the Salween and Irrawaddy in the Burmese sector of the region also could have provided home to many of the groups, some of which, again entered the Indian Territory from the eastern provinces of China, such as Yunnan into Burma and South East Asia and then entered Arunachal Pradesh and Assam over different ages in later times. The myths on migration of tribes of Arunachal who possess rich traditional accounts orally transmitted from generation to generation also speak about such movements. Thus, it is evident that from around 1000 B.C. these Mongoloid speakers of the Tibeto-Burmese languages had got their preponderant influences over the Himalayan region of North Eastern India including Arunachal Pradesh.

The Myang Province of Tibet was the ancestral home of the Tanis (Adi, Apatani, Hill-Miri, Mishing, Nyishi and Tagin etc). It was located in the eastern Tibet which was inaccessible either from Tibet or China. It is said, Shrong Tsan Gampo, the king of Tibet of the Yarlung dynasty got married to the princess of Nepal, a diehard Buddhist in the early seventh century A.D. The Tibetan king after that got heavily influenced by her and hence declared Buddhism as the state religion which led to internal dissension in Tibet. It led to rebellion in Myang province too. The people of the province were animists and they rose into arms to protect and preserve their age- old culture and tradition against an alien religious belief. But the king Shrong Tsan Gampo sent troops and ousted the Tanis from Myang province. The Tanis left their ancestral home and settled down in Pemako Valley (Kham regions) of Tibet. Here, the Tanis and Taros lived in brotherhood. But in due course, due to growth of their number and shortage of arable land, quarrels began to crop up. The Taros came out victorious and the Tanis had to leave the country and move towards the southern slopes of the Himalayas.

It is known that the foundation of the Ahom dynasty and Ahom rule in Assam by Sukapha in 1228 A.D. laid the beginning of the medieval history of Arunachal Pradesh. Sukapha left his ancestral homeland (Maulung in Upper Myanmar) in 1215 A.D. after his quarrel with his brother. For thirteen years, from 1215 to 1228 A.D. he had to wander about the rugged hills of the Patkai range raiding occasionally on the Wancho and Nocte villages of Tirap district of Arunachal Pradesh on his mission to march towards Assam. He had to resort to cruel methods to subjugate his formidable enemies. He was able to cross Patkai through Pangchu pass to Khamjang, the country of the Shyams in Tirap. He again crossed a river called Khamnamjang in rafts and came to the Nonyang Lake. Frightful enemies surrounded all around him. But his ghastly and barbaric perpetration towards them compelled them to submission to him. Leaving one of his nobles called Khamjangia Gohain, accompanying him in his entire journey to rule over the conquered country, Sukapha proceeded to Dikrong, Khamnangnangpu and reached Namrup in Assam in 1228 A.D.

Ahom-Tangsa Relations

The first ever contact of any sort between the Ahoms and the tribes of Arunachal after the establishment of the Ahom administration in Assam in 1228 A.D. can be traced back to 1487 A.D. when the Tangsas living presently in the Changlang district of Arunachal raided the Ahom territory during the reign of the Ahom king Susenpha (1439-1488) who in retaliation personally attacked and routed them but lost one hundred and forty of his personnel in the battle. In 1488, Subenpha (1488-1493) succeeding Susenpha sent an expedition afresh against the Tangsas. They became not only victorious but became successful in getting the Ahom General beheaded. But the second expedition led to Ahom's victory and the Tangsas refused to sign any treaties with the Ahoms.

Mention may be made, the Ahoms adopted separate policies i.e., Policy of Conciliation and Policy of Subjugation towards each tribe according to its behaviours, strength, urgency of circumstances and its location. The tribes who lived on the frontier of the Ahom Kingdom had different languages and customs. Moreover, they lived in isolation. Their economy was not self- sufficient and their hill produces were not enough for their livelihood. So, in order to fulfill their requirements, they used to come down to the plains near the foothills. They came either to exchange their produces or to plunder the people living in the plain areas. Sometimes they carried away not only crops and cattle but also the people to enslave them. But generally the Ahoms preferred the policy of conciliation towards the tribes. The tribes of Arunachal who could be brought to different kind of relations by the Ahoms were the Adis, Mishmis, Akas, Nyishis, Khamptis, Singphos, Noctes and Bhutias (Monpas and Shedukpens). Let us now discuss when such relations of what nature could be developed.

Ahom-Adi Relations

The Adis living in the East and West Siang, eastern border of the Upper Subansiri and the south western part of the Dibang valley of present Arunachal, came into contact with the Ahoms when the Chutiya Kingdom was annexed to the Ahom territory in 1523 A.D. during the reign of Suhungmung or Dihingia Raja (1497-1539). The Adis mostly occupied the hill- country between rivers Dihang and Dibang. The river Dibang separated them from the cultivated country of the Brahmaputra valley. The Miris, who occupied the plains and lower hills along the north bank of the Brahmaputra from the Subansiri River on the west as far as Dihang River on the east, were considered as the dependants and runaway slaves of the Adis.

The main thrust of the Ahom policy towards their neighbours was based on the well known four principles of Indian political philosophy viz. *Sama-dana-danda-veda*, i.e., establishment of relations of equal status, establishment of subservient suzerainty, a wording of punishments and driving wedges among neighbours.[3] The Adis also forced the Beehs- the Hindu gold- washers and fish- catchers, employed by the Ahoms who went to collect gold and fish from Dibang, Dihang and other tributaries of the Brahmaputra to give them frequent offerings to reconcile the Adis. The Ahoms did not initiate any specific action against them. During the reign of Pratap Singha (1603-41) the Ahom administration rather recognised their claims and some of the villages in the plains were given to them whose residents were to work for their Adi masters. Against such privilege granted to them the Adis were supposed to pay an annual tribute to the Ahom government.

Ahom-Mishmi Relations

Various groups of Mismis (such as the Idus or Chulikata, the Taraon or Digaru and the Kamanar Miju) lived in the hills to the east of the Adis (presently inhabiting the Lohit, Anjaw and Dibang Valley districts of Arunachal). After the annexation of the Chutia kingdom the Ahoms came in contact with the Mishmis. The first reference of the contact of the Mishims with Ahoms can be traced back to the reign of Sutyinpha (1644- 48) who constructed a *Mishmi- garh* (rampart) to resist the Mishmi - raiders. However, the *Buranji* gives only one reference of a Mishmi raid on the Ahom territory in 1675 during the reign of Ramdhvaj Singha (1673-1675) whereby the Mishmis killed four Ahom priests in the Deoghar (temple) in Sadiya and with the help of the Doanias (said to be the half-breeds of the Singphos) compelled the Ahom forces led by the Sadiya Khowa Gohain (an Ahom officer looking after the Sadiya frontier) to retreat. Later on the Mishmis submitted on the arrival of a stronger force under the Bar Phukan (an Ahom officer looking after the civil and military administration). The *Sadiya Stone Pillar Inscription* (probably inscribed in about 1687) issued by the Dihingia Bargohain (the Ahom overlord of the Sadiya region) confirms a settlement between the Ahoms and Mishmis. The Mishmis were asked to pay tribute to the Sadiya Khowa Gohain.

Ahom-Aka Relations

The Akas (or Hrusso) who lived in the hills north of Charduar were divided into two clans- the *Hazari Khowas* (eaters at a thousand hearths) and the *Kapachors* (thieves who lurk amid the cotton plants). These Akas were granted the right of Posa by the Ahoms in the Charduar areas in the plains. According to the records of 1825, the Akas were entitled to receive from each house of their allotted Paiks, "one portion of a female dress, one bundle of cotton thread and one handkerchief". The Kapachors were more troublesome. They used to raid the Darrang region. Their leader Taghi Raja used to collect dues from Charduar forcibly. He was suppressed by the British in 1842.

Ahom-Nyishi Relations

The Ahoms came into contact with the Nyishis (the Ahom and British records speak them Daflas) after the annexation of the Chutia Kingdom (1522-23). They were living mostly in the hills north of Na-Duar (nine passes) in Darrang and Che-Duar (six passes) in Lakhimpur. They proved to be the most formidable for the Ahom administration. In 1562 the Nyishis invaded the plains during the reign of Sukhampa, the Khora Raja (1552-1603) who adopted defensive measures by constructing forts and appointing a new officer called Salal

Gohain to keep them in check. King Pratap Singha (1603-1641) has also got constructed a fort called the Dafla Garh in Darrang as a sequel to an utter failure of the Ahom expedition against the Western Dafla (Nyishis) in 1614. Pratap Singha even granted *Posa* to the Nyishis in order to conciliate them. The Nyishi raids on the plains still continued. King Sutyinpha's (1644-1648) expedition in 1646, and King Sunyatpha's (1670-1672) expedition in 1672 against them did not prove successful.

King Gadadhar Singha (1681- 96) got the Daflas pacified by placing a number of people, known as the Dafla- Bahatiyas under them. King Rudra Singha (1696 -1714) was also successful in invoking them to send their troops in his proposed invasion of Bengal. The Western Daflas came down from the hills north of Darrang, about six hundred in number, to join Darrang to join the Ahom army. But after Rudra Singha's death in 1714, their relationship again turned hostile. King Siva Singha (1714 - 44) subdued the Daflas in 1717. King Rajendra Singha (1751- 69) also tried to prevent the Dafla raids. He got forts erected and put restrictions on Daflas entering to markets. They suffered badly due to the ban. Finally, agreement could be signed by which they were allowed to levy 'Posa' on condition of their refraining from the act of aggression. From an account of 13th May 1825, we come to know that every year from every ten houses of Dafla-Bahatiyas, the Nyishis were entitled to receive one double cloth, one single cloth, one handkerchief, one dao, ten heads of horned cattle and four seers of salt.[4]

Ahom-Khampti Relations

The Khamptis migrated to the borders of Sadiya in Assam from the ancient kingdom of Mung- Mau or Pong in Burma in 1740s. Being the close kinsmen of the Ahoms, the Khamptis were allowed to settle on the banks of Tengapani River in 1751. They used to come to the Sadiya market to buy and sell various articles. They took advantage of the weak position of the Ahom king due to Moamaria rebellion and joined their hands with the Moamaria revolutionaries. In 1794 the

Khamptis crossed the river Brahmaputra, ousted the Sadiya Khowa Gohain, the Ahom Governor of Sadiya and established their rule over Sadiya with two chiefs namely Burha Raja and Deka Raja. In 1799, they along with *Pani Naras* and *Phakials* (other sects of Shans) and the Miris, Mishmis and the Abors (Adis) challenged the Ahom authority during the reign of Kamaleshwar Singha (1795-1811). The Burha Raja of the Khamptis came down with a large army and waited with hostile intentions at Nibok in the north bank of the river Brahmaputra but got badly defeated by the large Ahom army sent by Purnananda Burha Gohain, the Ahom Prime Minister. The Ahom rule was restored in Sadiya. The Khamptis remained quiet for some time but certainly caused trouble to the Ahoms during to the Burmese invasion of Assam (1816-1824).

Ahom-Singpho Relations

The Singphos drove out the Khamptis from Tengapani and settled in the Upper Burhi Dihing in Namrup. We get the accounts of the presence of Singphos during the reign of Kamaleshwar Singha (1795-1811) when the Moamaria rebellion was in full swing. The Singphos became a partner of the Moamarias and the Burmese invaders and raised their voice against the Ahoms. They even raided many villages. The Ahom Prime Minister Purnananda Burha Gohain tried to conciliate the Singpho chief Bichanong by presenting him an Ahom girl named Rangili. Bichanong presented Rangili to the Burmese King in order to strengthen ties with him. But the agreement did not last long. During the Burmese invasion of Assam, the Singphos made a number of attacks on the villages in the plains, carried away a number of slaves and reduced the population of the village in the eastern parts considerably. About three thousand of the Assamese subjects were recovered from the captivity of the Singphos by Capt. Neufville, the first Political Agent of Upper Assam.

Ahom-Nocte Relations

The Noctes got settled in the Tirap district of Arunachal Pradesh from as early as the twelfth or thirteenth century. They came in contact with the Ahoms when the latter were going to Assam for settlement. Ownership right over the salt- springs and wells was basic reason of conflict between the Noctes and Ahoms. The Ahom Buranjis record that the Ahom seized a salt-well in Mohang in 1536 and in due course, enjoyed either exclusive rights on several such wells or share in the salt produced in them. In 1692, during the reign of the Ahom King Gadadhar Singha (1681-1696), the Noctes raided salt mine and killed 20 persons. Attacks and counter-attacks continued from both sides. A confrontation came into being in 1700 whereby both sides suffered. They also raided the plains of Assam in 1807 during the reign of Kamaleshwar Singha (1795-1811). Mention may be made here that the Nocte- Ahom relationships did not always base on friction and enmity; but friendship, commercial and cultural intercourse also existed between them.

Ahom-Bhutia Relations

Bhutan had close contact with the plains through several *duars* (passes). There were eleven such *duars* in Bengal and seven in Assam (two in Darrang and five in Kamrup). The Assam *duars* were claimed by the Ahom government. But in eighteenth century, the weak Ahom rulers made over the Darrang and Kamrup *duars* to the Bhutias in return for an annual payment of tribute in the form of yak-tails, ponies, musk, gold dust, blankets and knives. So long as the tribute was paid, the *duars* were to remain under the Bhutias for seven months (December to June) and for the rest five months (July to November) they were to be surrendered to the Ahom government. This curious arrangement led to many types of troubles and quarrels between the authorities of the Ahoms and Bhutan. The Monpas of the Bhutia stock were under the governor of Tawang and the direct control of the *Sat Rajas* who controlled the *Kuriapara duar*. They used to come to Udalguri fair in the Darrang district of Assam. Their relations had been mostly peaceful with the Ahoms. Similarly, the Sherdukpens (also of the Bhutia stock) also collected tribute from the plains. The British government stopped these privileges enjoyed by the tribes.

The above Ahom- tribal relationship goes to suggest that the different tribes of Arunachal had their relations with the Ahom administration ranging from the fag end of fifteenth century to the beginning of ninetieth century, i.e., from 1487 whereby Tangsas could be found raiding the plains of Assam during the reign of the Ahom ruler Susenpha (1439-1488) to 1807 whereby the Noctes raiding the plains of Assam during the reign of the Ahom ruler Kamaleshwar Singha (1795-1811).

Modern period

The modern history of Arunachal Pradesh begins with the annexation of Assam by the British in 1826 after the Treaty of Yandaboo which opened up a new chapter in the history of North East India as whole. The previous regime of the Ahoms lasted over the Brahmaputra valley for over six centuries (1228-1826). By the end of eighteenth century the kingdom was in the crater of an internal rebellion, which weakened it substantially. The Burmese desire for eastward expansion fuelled by royal intrigue in the Ahom Court led to the Burmese invasion in 1819. Ravaged by the Burmese insurrection the weakened Ahom monarch turned to the East India Company seeking its aid to deal with the situation. The Anglo– Burmese War which was ensued got concluded with the signing of the Treaty of Yandaboo. The legacy of the undefined and bedeviled relations of the Ahom kings with the tribes of Arunachal was over. The British stepped into the shoes of Ahoms and inherited from the latter a legacy of relationship with the hill tribes of present Arunchal Pradesh.

The British attention on the North Eastern India got more and more focused once the discoveries of tea bushes in 1823, coal and petroleum in 1825 in Upper Assam could be made in the wake of First Anglo- Burmese war. It was also noticed that the territories in the foothills were extremely rich containing valuable forest products like timer and ivory and fertile land in the area would produce surplus revenue if the farmers could be induced to take up cultivation. The British also contemplated to explore a trade route to China through China as during the period Nepal, Bhutan and Burma were suspicious of the British and averse to provide any outlet to them through their territories. Hence, it was not possible for them to leave these foot-hills in a state of confusion and allow the tribesmen to raid them every now and then. It was, therefore, thought best to follow a policy of reconciliation, backed by the display of force when necessary towards the hill people of Arunachal.

The initial British policy towards the tribes was to protect the British tea plantation and extraction of rich minerals, oil fields and forest wealth in Upper Assam without any confrontation with the tribesmen of Arunachal Pradesh. Therefore, they continued the payment of posa to the hill tribes of Arunachal as existed during the days of the Ahom. This British policy of appeasement failed in due course of time as the tribesmen carried on feudatory incursions into the plains of Assam in order to punish the refractory subjects who moved away from the detriment of the hill masters and who refused to pay taxes defying the age-old traditions. On the issue of jurisdiction over the Assamese subjects the tribesmen of Arunachal Pradesh used to clash with the British culminating into a series of eventful wars leading to the final fall of tribes getting defeated decisively in the Anglo-Adi war of 1911. Arunachal after this came officially under the British rule although territories remained unadministered under the British policy of 'Loose Political Control' over the tribes nevertheless the British India's territorial boundary nominally extended up to the Mac Mahon Line. The British Government found the state unproductive and economically unviable and hence took little effort to augment development.

Let us have little discussion on the British relations with some of the tribes of Arunachal Pradesh so that we can have sound justification on the periodisation-issue of the history of Arunachal that is to take place in the chapter follows.

British- Monpa Relations (1830-1880)

The Monpas living presently in the West Kameng and Tawang districts of Arunachal were known as the Bhutias of Kuriapara Duars and were under the rule of the chiefs, called the Sat Rajas[5] who were subordinates of the Tawang Raja, a tributary of Lhasa (Tibet). Between 1830 and 1840, since the Monpas put the British in trouble, the latter decided to annex the Kuriapara Duars (passes) of Darrang of Assam and restricted the movements of the Monpas. Thus, hard pressed, they became ready for an agreement. In 1843-44 the Sat Rajas (Seven Chiefs) and the agents of the Governor of Tawang made an agreement with Captain Gordon and formally gave up all claims to the lands of the Kuriapara Duars (including the posa) in lieu of an annual grant of ₹ 5000.[6] In 1852 the British relation with the Sat Rajas got little strained due to duplicity of one of the *Gellings* who were appointed by the Governor of Tawang as supervision of the Sat Rajas. However, in 1853 a fresh treaty could be signed by which friendly relations between them could be restablished.[7]

Since then British relations with the Bhutias remained perfectly amicable. In 1872-73 the boundary between Assam and the Monpa country was demarcated from the Deoshan River on the west to Rowta River on the east. The restriction placed on the intercourse with the hills under the Inner Line Regulation of 1873 which came into force in 1875 gave rise to some complaint in 1876-77, but the grievances were met by the issue of passes to all persons bona fide engaged in supplying the hill men. In 1878, the provisions of the Regulation were suspended along their frontier and in 1880 the Deputy Commissioner, Darrang (Assam) settled a quarrel between the Monpas and Bhutanese of Bhutan proper. Since then the Monpas remained peaceful ever.

British- Sherdukpen Relations (1836-1873)

The Sherdukpens or Thongjis of the Bhutia stock who had their abode in Rupa and Shergaon in the present West Kameng district were under the Sat Rajas and were active in

Char Duar (Four Passes) areas with one Dorjee Raja of Rupa being the most prominent. They used to collect tributes from the plains. After the British annexation of Assam, the British signed an agreement with them in February, 1836 by which Captain Matthie, the Collector and Magistrate of Darrang resumed the right of direct collection and paid them ₹ 2526-27 as compensation on that account. This payment was however, stopped in 1839 when the Sherdukpens murdered Madhu Saikia, a British subject in a Charduar village. After negotiations, they were pardoned and eventually a reduced allowance of ₹ 1740 (lesser than the original due ₹ 2526-27) was granted to them. In 1872-73 the southern boundary of the Sherdukpens was laid down from the Rowta River on the west to Gabru (Belsiri) River in the east. They objected in the beginning and demanded some lands in the plains. But in the end, they accepted the boundary line after signing an agreement in February 1878 with the Deputy Commissioner of Darrang.

British –Aka Relations (1825-1914)

The Akas living presently in the West Kameng district constantly appeared in the British Records as the Hazarikhowas and Kapachors. The British Revenue Records of February 5, 1825 show that it was to the Hazarikhowa Akas that the British Government at the time of annexation of Assam granted the right to collect Posa. They were entitled to receive from each house of their allotted khels (tribute paying settlement) one portion of female dress, one bundle of cotton thread and one cotton handkerchief. Perhaps they used to give a part of their collection to the Kapachors who had not been granted such right. The system being found cumbersome was replaced by David Scott, the first Political Officer in terms of commutation of the collection of dues in kind by the tribes by a system of payment in cash. The Akas agreed to forego their collection against an annual payment of ₹ 175 by the British Government.

The British Government had no good relations with the Kapachor Akas. Their leader Taghi Raja had been collecting dues from Duars forcibly and also murdered an official of Charduar. For this David Scott had declared them outlaw. In 1829, Taghi Raja had a dispute with the Hazarikhowas and then fled to Assam, where he was captured and sent to the Guwahati jail. In 1832, he was released. In 1835, he burnt the Assam Light Infantry outpost at Balipara and killed seventeen people. The Hazarikhowas, suspected of alliance with Kapachors, were not granted annual payment. When the British Government decided to send a punitive expedition to the Aka Hills, Taghi Raja in 1842 surrendered. On an oath of good behaviour, he was made a stipendiary of ₹ 20. Following him many other Aka chiefs also accepted stipends in 1844 and 1848. But their demand to increase the stipend amount continued. By 1857, the British Government increased the stipends up to ₹ 668.

A fresh trouble began when the British Government tried to demarcate boundary line between the Darrang district and the Aka hills in 1872-73. The Akas wanted some revenue free land in the foot hills and hence granted 36 puras of land. The Akas were satisfied and the boundary was demarcated in 1874-75. The Kapachor Akas did not accept the boundary line wholeheartedly. In 1883, the Akas captured Lakhidhar and two others who were guiding a party for collection of specimens from the hills for Calcutta exhibition.[8] Lakhidhar died in detention. In the cold season of 1883-84, Chandi, the brother of Medhi Raja, the Aka chief, raided the Balipara Forest Range Office. After this incident, the British Government sent for the first time a big expedition to the Aka hills led by Captain Maxwell, the Political Officer. Despite their resistance movement the Akas got defeated. The Chief Commissioner of Assam directed the Deputy Commissioner of Darrang to continue the blockade of the hills till the surrender of Medhi.

In 1888, many Aka chiefs submitted. Medhi, the Aka chief accepted the foot hills as the boundary between their hills and the British territory. The posa was restored in 1890 to them on the promise of good behaviour. In 1900 the Akas demanded a sum of ₹ 3000 from a merchant of Balipara for taping rubber in their hills. The Deputy Commissioner of Darrang since interfered, things could be settled. The British relation with Akas remained peaceful after this event. The Aka hills were included in the western section of the North East Frontier in 1913. In the same year G.A. Nevill, the Political Officer of the Western Section led a promenade through their hills, explored and surveyed over 400 square miles of territory of the Miji and Aka hills. The Aka hills were brought under the British control in 1914.

British- Nyishi Relations (1825-1911)

The British relation with the Nyishis presently living in the East Kameng and Subansiri districts of Arunachal can be traced back to a date of May 13, 1825 when it was found that the Nyishis were entitled to receive from every ten houses of Bohotias (Assamese ryots) one double cloth, one single cloth, one handkerchief, one dao, ten heads of horned cattle and four seers of salt. The British Government faced problem from the side of the Nyishis. In 1835 they committed a raid on plains and carried off several British subjects, but rescued later after negotiation. The Nyishis left their right of collecting posa from the paiks and agreed to receive the articles of posa from the revenue office of the village. But the Nyishis of the Na Duar (nine passes) did not accept the agreement since they treated the paiks (ryots) as their hereditary slaves.[9] In 1838-1839 they troubled the plains much. In 1852 the posa was finally commuted for a monthly payment of money.

In 1870, the hill Nyishis attacked on the Nyishi village on plains in search of an absconding slave. In the same year, one Nyishi village attacked the other due to a marriage issue. One more raid started in 1872-73 when about 300 hill Nyishis (Tagins) attacked the village of Amtolla of Darrang. The British Government took all these raids seriously and blocked their passes to the east of the Darrang and along the Lakhimpur frontier, but proved futile. Things could be settled after a military expedition was sent into the hills in 1874-1875. In the early part of twentieth century, the British tried to make direct contact with them of the interior hills. In 1911, a survey party (known as the Miri Mission) visited many villages of the Nyishi hills and collected important information. In the same year, the Nyishi hills got included in the western section of the North East Frontier.

British- Apatani Relations (1874-1944)

The Apatanis who reside presently in the Apatani valley of the Subansiri area of Arunachal have been described as an enterprising and industrious tribe. Major Graham's report on the "Dafla Expedition of 1874-75" referred to the Apatanis for the first time. They were known to the British as Anka Miris, sometimes as Tenai Miris. In fact, they could not come in contact with the plains as the Nyishi lived in the lower region bordering Assam.[10] As their contact with outside world was limited their land was also not visited by any enterprising European till 1889, when H. M. Crowe, the Manager of the Joyhing Tea Estate visited the Apatani plateau. Even Alexander Mackenzie did not mention about them in his famous monograph *British Relations with the Tribes of the North East Frontier*. In 1893 Captain Dun escorted by Crowe visited the Apatani area. A German explorer Herr von Ehlers also visited the valley in 1895. The British recorded them as gentle and peace loving.

The British- Apatani had been very cordial except on one occasion on November 8, 1896 when a 'Tarbotia Miri' (Hill Miri) named Padu and his stepson, Tapak were murdered near Mr H.M. Crowe's tea garden at Kadam within the Inner Line and four of his household taken captive. Mr F.C. Henniker, the Deputy Commissioner of Lakhimpur confirmed the offenders as "Apa Tanangs" or "Anka Miris'. An expedition against this incident got materialised under Captain C.R. Row associated by R.B. McCabe, the Inspector General of Police as the Political Officer which reached the Apatani valley on February 14, 1897. The expedition proved successful since it was able to recover the captives as well as the gun of H.M. Crow. The British- Apatani relations never turned sour after that. In 1912, the member of the Miri Mission also visited the Apatani valley and collected important information regarding the valley. In 1944 C. von Furer Haimendorf was appointed the special officer of the Subansiri region who visited the Apatani valley many times and had a good rapport with them.

British- Adi Relations (1825-1911)

The British relations with the Adis living presently in the East, West Upper Siang districts and in the Dibang Valley of Arunachal Pradesh, can be traced back to November 22,1825 which Captain Bedford visited Pasighat, deputed by the authorities of East India Company at Calcutta to explore a trade route to China through North East Frontier (Arunachal Pradesh), though officially stated different, i.e., to discover the source of the Brahmaputra River and collect some geographical information about North East India.[11] Lt. R.Wilcox also met some of the Adi chiefs who had arrived to make annual collections from the northern bank of Brahmaputra on November 28, 1825 on his way to Subansiri to explore the country. Negotiations and relations of various sorts also continued from 1826 to 1830 between the Adis and British.

So far the Adis were not so hostile. In 1836 about two hundred Adis came down and offered to settle on the Dibang. They were ready to accept the British criminal jurisdiction, but objected to pay taxes. The British desired to encash the Adis' strength against Khamptis, Singphos and Mishmis. In 1840, the Adis rendered them help against those tribes. In 1847, Captain Vetch, the Political Agent released some of the Adi captives arrested earlier on the issue of gold washers and fishermen. In January 1858, the Minyong Adis of Kabang village attacked on the Beheeah village of Sangajan (in the north of Barahmaputra), very close to Dibrugarh leading to the killing of twenty-one people. An expedition was sent in 1858, and another in 1859. Situation became normal by November 1862, when eight khels of Minyong Adis concluded an agreement with the Deputy Commissioner of Lakhimpur by which they accepted the British sovereignty up to the foothills and promised not to disturb the British subjects. Agreements too soon followed with the Kabang and Padam Adis. But they did not like the British to have close eyes of them. In 1877, the payment of stipends in kind was stopped and cash payment was fixed. In 1882, J.F. Needham was appointed the Assistant Political Officer and posted at Sadiya. Several Adi raids took place in the 1890s. The government stopped paying stipends to them.

From the beginning of the twentieth century the British Government became more concerned about the independent status of the frontier hills. Series of missions were sent to the hills in order to check the Chinese activities in Tibet, the Lhasa Mission of 1904 being the first. Noel Williamson, who was posted in 1905 as the Assistant Political Officer at Sadiya, visited the Mishmi and Adi hills and had a close watch on the Chinese activities. In 1907, he went up to Rima in Lohit Valley and Kabang in Adis hills. In 1908, he visited the Pasi, Minyong and some Galo villages around Pasighat. In 1911, he again visited the Mishmi hills up to Walong and noticed some Chinese activities at Rima. In March 1911, once again he visited the same hills accompanied by Dr J.D. Gregorson and more than forty other people. On March 18, 1911, Williamson and his party reached Rotung from where they went up to Pangi. On 30 March, he left the Pangi camp, leaving Dr Gregorson there. On the same day the Adis of Kabang and Babuk came to Pangi and killed Dr Gregorson. Then they followed Williamson and he was also killed at Komsing on 31 March 1911.

The murder of Williamson resulted in the Adi war of 1911. This was also proved to be a serious challenge for the British Government. For the safety of frontier and tea gardens, military expedition was sent to the Adis hills in 1911 led by Major General H. Bower. It had to establish British military superiority in the hills; to punish the culprits of massacre; to get indemnity for the massacre; to explore and survey the hills and also to find possibility of demarcating boundary line between India and Tibet. The British captured and destroyed many Adi villages such as, Korang, Rotung and Kabang etc. The murderers of Williamson and his party were captured, tried and punished. In this way British supremacy was established in the region.

British- Mishmi Relations (1825-1914)

Lohit and Dibang Valley districts are at present the abode of the Mishmis. They were engaged in extensive trade with the outside world, the Digaru or Taraon Mishmis had trade intercourse with Tibet and the Chulikatas traded with plains of Assam.[12] From the very beginning they did not like to receive the foreigners as Lt. Burlton observed after his visit to the Mishmi hills in 1825.[13] Dr Griffith also reported the same in 1826. This view could be perhaps on the fact than an Indian *fakir*, Paramanand Acharya (1848) and French missionary M. Krick (1854) were murdered by them while they were passing through this country. An expedition under Lt. Eden was sent to capture the culprits. He was caught, tried and hanged.

The Idu (Chulikata) Mishmis used to trouble the British a lot while coming down to plains of Assam for trade. They used to get themselves involved in frequent raids between 1855 and 1866. The British launched strategy to block them. As a sequel, the British provided arms and lands to Khamptis who would resist their raids. In 1866 a trade fair was organised at Sadiya to ban such raids where the Mishmis exchanged their textiles, daos, musk, ornaments, rubber and Mishmi teeta for salt and other things with the other communities of Arunachal like the Khamptis, Singphos and Adis. During 1877-78 Woodthorpe visited the Dibang valley. British outposts were created at Nizamghat and Bhismaknagar. In 1880, the Kaladoi (Idu Mishmi) formally declared their allegiance to the British.[14] In 1889-1900, J. F. Needham, Assistant Political Officer of Sadiya led an expedition against the Bebajiya clan of Mishmis for their unruly activities.

Due to the Chinese activities in remote Mishmi hills and the murder of Noel Williamson in 1911, the British Government became more concerned about the security of the frontiers. In November 1911, a Mishmi Mission was sent under W.C.M. Dundas for the purpose. In fact, a type of British protection began in the Mishmi hills after this mission and subsequent explorations in the hills. In 1914, the Mishmi hills were included in the Central and Eastern sections of the frontier.

British- Khampti Relations (1824-1844)

The Khamptis lived below the Mishmi hills to the south on the Brahmaputra and between Mishmis and the Singphos. Records say, in 1797-1800, the Barasiriagis revolted in Sadiya. The Khamptis joined them and crossed the Brahmaputra and ousted the Assamese governor of Sadiya.[15] The Khampti chief ruled like an independent prince. The Khamptis rendered material help to the British Government in 1824 in their campaign against the Singphos. That is why, David Scot, the Governor General's Agent recognised Chow-Salan, the son of Chow-Mu-ngan Lung as the lawful ruler of Sadiya and permitted him to collect poll tax from the Assamese of the Sadiya area on certain conditions. In 1830, the Khamptis under the leadership of Piyali Phukan contemplated a revolted against the British supported by the Singphos, Nagas, Khasis, Garos and the Mataks.

The British relation with them remained peaceful. The British Government even gave permission to settle a new group of Khampti immigrants in 1835. The first conflict between them appeared on a land dispute between the Matak and Khampti chiefs in 1838. Before the truce could be brought about, the Khamptis forcibly occupied the land. So the British removed the chief from Sadiya and his post was abolis hed which resulted ultimately in an attack of the Khamptis on the British on January 19, 1839 killing Colonel White, the Political Agent and a number of British soldiers. An immediate expedition was sent. The Khamptis fled to the Mishmi hills. They were tactically pursued, but they could not be submitted before December 1843. By 1844 the Khamptis surrendered. After this incident Sadiya and Matak countries were directly brought under the British rule. Since then they remained peaceful and were included in the Eastern Section of North East Frontier.

British- Singpho Relations (1825-1843)

Presently the Singphos live in the Changlang and Lohit districts of Arunachal. Raising a strong force with the

Assamese slaves at backdrop the Singphos were considered the most powerful tribe bordering Assam by 1825. They attacked the Khampti chief of Sadiya and virtually expelled the Khamptis from there. The British compelled them to come to terms. By June 1825 the Burmese appeared on the Patkai and started occupying the Singpho villages of Bisa and Duffa Gams. The British expelled them from all these areas and the Singpho chiefs also surrendered. In 1826 sixteen Singpho chiefs made agreement with the British. Many still were left. In 1830, some of them along with the Khamptis tried to expel the British from Sadiya. But their attempt failed. In spite of agreement of 1826, many Singpho chiefs were still keeping large number of slaves because their economy depended on slave labour.

In 1843 there broke out a powerful Singpho revolt involving almost all Singpho chiefs on the issues of the encroachment on the lands and privileges of Singphos and punishment given to some Singphos by the local officers. The British suppressed the revolt and all the chiefs surrendered. After this, they remained almost peaceful. In 1914, the Singpho tract was included in the Eastern Section of the North East Frontier.

British- Nocte Relations (1841-1900)

The Noctes living presently in the Tirap district of Arunachal were brought to relations under the British when Captain Brodie, the Principal Assistant to Governor General's Agent visited the Nocte area in 1841-42. There were internal feuds in the Nocte groups of Namsangias, Borduaris and Paniduaris which disturbed the British peace in the plains. In November 1853, the Namsangia chiefs demanded tribute from several villages ruled by the Chief of Borduaris. In 1884, the Namsangias quite good in number at that time were still at feud with Borduaries.[16] In 1888 a group of Namsangias carried away six persons from Dilli village and put one among them to death. They were all brought to a peaceful agreement. Despite this, in 1900 two Nocte groups got again involved in a clash. The British Government started administrative control in those areas to maintain peace and order. Regular administration was established in the area by the formation of Tirap Frontier Tract in 1943, under the charge of a Political Officer.

British- Wancho Relations (1841-1875)

The Wanchos also live in the Tirap district of Arunachal. They used to carry on a most profitable trade in slaves and oppressed all ryots in the neighbourhood. The greed for gain led to endless feuds between the villages and tribes with the object of carrying off slaves as prisoners to be sold in Sibsagar, Assam. This put the British in trouble. The British refrained the Wanchos from doing so after an arrangement made in 1841- 42. In 1841-42, Captain Brodie also visited the Wancho villages of Banfera, Joboka, Jaktong, Tablung and Changno. In 1844, the Bor Mihunias, a group of Wanchos attacked the Banfera village which resulted in outrages in the areas close to the border of Sibsagar district in 1851 and 1869. In 1875, a big survey party visited the Wancho areas under Lt. Holcombe. But the Wanchos killed about eight men of the survey party including Holcombe. Hence, the British closed the entry of Wanchos to the plains. They remained isolated for a long time.

British- Tangsa Relations (1836-1910)

The Tangsas are said to have migrated from the Patkai and settled in Tirap. They came into contact with the British in 1836. The British explorer made mention of a trade route to Burma passing through the Tangsa country (Namchik Valley). Though peaceful in nature, the Tangsas occasionally raided and kidnapped the British subjects. To keep them in check, an outpost was opened at Tikhak and the post at Ledo was reinforced in 1897. They have been reported kidnapping tea labourers during 1899 -1900. Their raids continued up to 1934.

The above discussion capsuled under modern period of history of Arunachal suggests that the British tribal relationship started as early as 1825 once the British had footage in Assam after the Anglo- Burmese War. One thing which seems to be very transparent in this context is that it was the Ahom legacy bequeathed to the British to maintain their nexus with the tribes of the North East in as insular way as had been maintained so far with Arunachal posing no extraordinary exception before them. A patchwork policy could only be initiated, executed and maintained. The incessant tribal threats in terms of frequent raids on the plains of Assam resorting sometimes to the British objectionable phenomena like loot, kidnap and murder often put them in an administrative mesh. Given the geographical and topographical hazards and nature's often unpredictable challenges that the then Arunachal threw before them, for a trading company like that of the British East India Company which had profit as one of its cynosure- policies to spend pies on journey, survey, expedition and above all on maintaining relations with tribes living beyond their comfort-eye-contact perception to the exclusion of the phenomena mentioned above, has to be construed critically. Of course, things started changing with the onset of the twentieth century. British orientation towards Arunachal got a preponderant importance once the Chinese frowning eyes on the north of present Arunachal started distracting their comfort-eye-contact perception. The murder of Noel Williamson in 1911 seconded it and alarmed them to streamline a clear-cut border policy towards Arunachal.

References

1. N. Lego, *Ancient and Medieval History of Arunachal Pradesh (From the Earliest times to 1824)*, Itanagar, 2006, pp. 8-9.
2. *Ibid.*
3. D. Pandey and B.K. Tripathy, *A Comprehensive History of Arunachal Pradesh*, Pasighat, 1997, p. 241.
4. *Ibid*, p. 246.
5. M.L. Bose, *British Policy in the North East Frontier Agency*, New Delhi, 1979, p. 48.
6. C. U. Aitchison, *A Collection of Treaties, Engagements and Sanads,* Vol. XII, 1973 (Reprint), Government of India Central Publication Branch, pp. 119-120 and pp. 142-143.
7. A. Mackenzie, *History of the Relations of the Government with the Hill Tribes of the North- East Frontier of Bengal*, Calcutta, 1884, p.17.
8. Bose, *op.cit,* p. 57.

9. Mackenzie, *op.cit,* p. 28.
10. N. Lego, *Modern History of Arunachal Pradesh (1825-2006)*, Itanagar, 2006, p. 19.
11. *Ibid*, p. 22.
12. Mackenzie, *op.cit,* p. 47.
13. Bose, *op.cit,* p. 75.
14. Mackenzie, *op.cit,* p. 52.
15. G. Barua, Ahom Buranji, Guwahati, 1930, pp. 364-65.
16. Lego, *Modern History of Arunachal Pradesh (1825-2006), op.cit,* p. 100.

Chapter - 4

Periodisation and Problem

History is truth and truth is history. Is there anything left in between these two phenomena?[1] Certainly not. If the former is the sum- totality of the latter, the latter is equally the byproduct of the former. Both of them stand in congruence with each other. An attempt of fragmentation certainly leads to distortion. A distortion in truth or history reduces its totality asking the bias and prejudices to crop up. If it is so, then truth is not truth and that history is no way a history as we presume to be. Against such a backdrop periodising history is bound to invite debate in the phenomena of history. Similarly, periodisation in Indian history is a major problem faced by the historians. It is not an easy task as we think it to be, because history is a continuous process and it stands no way right to fix any particular time for the growth and decline of any civilisation. As E. H. Carr rightly puts, "History is a continuous process of interaction between the historian and his fact, an unending dialogue between the present and the past..."[2]

Periodisation is an attempt to categorise or divide historical time into discrete named blocks. It is a complex problem in history. History is in fact continuous and so all systems of periodisation are to some extent arbitrary. Almost every dynamic age is an "age of transition" as the cliche has it. It is nevertheless necessary to divide history in order to make sense of the past and to articulate changes over time.

Furthermore, different nations and cultures experience different histories and so do they require different models of periodisation. Periodising labels are being challenged and redefined all the time. Thus a historian may claim that there was no such thing as the Renaissance, while others will defend the concept. The reasons for this definitely seem to be complex. Periodising blocks not only inevitably overlap, but also seemingly contradict one another. Again, certain periodising concepts apply only under specific conditions.

However, for the sake of convenience, periodisation has been considered necessary and the historians have broadly divided the entire range of Indian history into three periods i.e., Hindu, Muslim and British or the more appropriate divisions like Ancient, Medieval and Modern. But there is no consensus among the historians to fix the border line between these periods. There is and will remain indeed some uncertainty over where the ancient period ends and the medieval begins, but the three-phase-periodisation theory is retained with a difference of a few centuries by one and all.

Such delineation of the three- phase history carries within it deeper social messages and biases and also has a definite influence on further historical researches. To begin with, there is an inherent assumption that there is indeed *an* Indian history which can be divided into so many phases. D. D. Kosambi, criticising the Soviet indologist D. A. Suleykin[3] says: "India is a not a mathematical point but a large country, a subcontinent with the utmost diversity of natural environment, language, historical development. Neither in the means of production nor in the stages of social development was there an overall homogeneity in the oldest times. Centuries must be allowed to pass before comparable stages of production and social relationships may be established between the Indus Valley, Bengal and Malabar. Even then, important differences remain which makes periodisation for India as a whole almost impossible, except with the broadest margins."[4]

What we construe here is that what begins with an unequivocal statement ends with a degree of ambiguity 'with broadest margins'. The idea of India itself is a product of long and incomplete history of integration of local and regional societies into larger political and cultural formations as the historian D. D. Kosambi puts it. Historians like Romila Thapar have occasionally dissected this to find a group of nuclear regions separated from each other by long distances of forest and pastoral tracts.[5] These nuclear regions (the Ganga Valley, Malwa, Raichur Doab, Andhra coastal plains, Saurashtra, Tamil coastal plains, Assam Valley, Odisha plains etc.) were characterised by peasant agriculture, settlement hierarchy, specialisation, a high degree of social stratification and above all state formation. Over time these nuclear regions were integrated politically and culturally. Hence, despite often emerging as autonomous socio-political units, they had similar political and social structures as well as religious and cultural norms. These in turn sought to integrate the societies around them into one social unit. Often what passes for Indian history is essentially the history of these nuclear regions, especially the Ganges Valley. The intervening vast spaces were inhabited by hunter-gatherer societies, tribal societies living on a mix of hunting, gathering, non-intensive cropping and animal husbandry and also tribes or bands practicing specialised crafts. The overwhelming presence of such societies had deep impact not only on spatialisation of the subcontinent but also on the course of its history even if read as the history of the nuclear regions. They simply cannot be treated as peripheral to Indian History as many historians have sought to do. Nor can they be taken as people without history – societies without change. They too went through processes of change and transformations but yet to come for reconstruction by the historians.

Differentiation at the regional level has been noticed even in the prehistoric period in the archaeological records left by the Mesolithic societies.[6] Regional entities and identities emerge stronger in the 'early medieval' period with distinct languages. These were necessarily focussed around the nuclear regions. Though these regional societies had strong interactions with each other, they often followed distinct courses of development.

Pan-regional states and religio-cultural traditions imposed a degree of uniformity in both social institutions and political structures between the regions. Still the regions developed distinct social and cultural formations beneath such uniformities with their own systems of production, labour forms, systems of subordination and control, property forms and forms of surplus production, appropriation and distribution. What characterised even these regional societies is the coexistence of multiple forms and relations of production and a symbiotic relation between them.[7]

These days it is possible not only to start from the regions but also to go into the individual societies that went to constitute the regions themselves. It is time to stand 'Indian History' on its head to put the regions and localities on the top. We need to look into the question of regions not only to examine the nature of diversities but also to explore spatialisation in the history of the subcontinent. Spatial diversities are not only a legacy of the past but are taken to have created and transformed in every epoch through the interaction of diverse societies and ecological niches. Urban spaces, rural spaces, the frontier forest and pastoral spaces, spaces in which state societies and caste societies flourished and spaces where tribal and other pre-peasant societies existed, patriarchal-patrilineal spaces and matrilineal-matrilocal spaces... these endless forms of spaces constantly interacted with each other to determine the nature of each other. The more evolved and complex state societies which have left us records of history have made their own constructions and stereotypes of these diverse spaces and we should take care to see these biases when we try to construct a history of spaces in the subcontinent.

One must also comment on the problem posed by delimiting the area of research to what is 'India' today. It is well known that one cannot understand the Kushana Empire or the Sultanate or the Mughal without studying Central Asian histories or for that matter understanding South Indian history without an excursus into South East Asian history or the North

East without going into East Asian or South East Asian histories.[8] Yet they seldom form a part of the problem of Indian university students.

The threefold division of Indian history into ancient, medieval and modern periods owes much to post Renaissance European self perception of its own history. The Renascent burghers were conscious of effecting a break with their own feudal past. Both the Renascent humanists and Enlightenment philosophers saw the feudal past as a period of darkness and decline of civilisation. This they contrasted with the 'ancient' classical Greco-Roman period which was to have registered a high watermark of civilisation. The prehistoric and pre-classical period (and non-classical regions) was largely ignored in this scheme. That is why, even Marx while accepting the label of 'ancient' for the classical ages introduced the notion of 'Asiatic' as a preceding epoch.[9] Of course, Marx did not share the notion of feudalism being a regression over the ancient period as he saw a progress in the labour form from slavery to serfdom.

When the British colonial administrator-historians and Utilitarian scholars studied Indian history, they advertently or inadvertently transferred the idea of tripartite division to Indian history. James Mill was probably the first to use the tripartite division to Indian history in the early nineteenth century.[10] Instead of the Ancient, Medieval and Modern categories he used 'Hindu, Muslim and British' periods. Prior to Mill the Romantic minded Orientalists like William Jones and later Max Muller valorised the 'Hindu period' through a study of Sanskrit texts. This was debunked by the Utilitarian scholars who spent much energy in negating any civilisational contribution of a non-European society. Nevertheless, the idea of a highly civilised Ancient India survived. These civilisational achievements were seen to be destroyed by the medieval barbarism of Muslim invaders much like the achievements of Classical Europe were 'destroyed' by the twin invasions of the barbarian tribes and Arab-Muslims. This was followed by the dark ages of the 'Muslim Rule' till the English East India

Company brought India to the threshold of modernity. Thus the tripartite division when applied to India had both the original connotations of European historiography and also an added element of using religion as indicators of epochs. Under this twin influence was founded the communal vision of Indian History which postulated a positive Hindu Ancient Period, a negative Muslim Medieval Period and a Modern Christian British Period. Indian history could be neatly divided into three phases – the Hindu Period lasting till 1190 A.D. followed by the Muslim Period with the founding of the Delhi Sultanate and ending with the Battle of Plassey (1757) which saw the beginning of British rule. The religion of the rulers was used as a marker or as an identifier because it was believed that Indian society especially the rural society was hardly in a position to change its nomenclature and the only change expected and felt was at the level of the rulers. There were disturbing factors like the extreme southern part never experiencing a stable Muslim rule, Rajasthan being ruled for long by Hindu rulers and Central and North East India either having no rulers or having no inclination to Islam in the so-called Muslim period. Still such tripartite division was too alluring to be set aside.

Periodisation is necessarily concerned with change. A society's history cannot be periodised if it did not undergo changes that too qualitative ones. Thus even while it was possible to divide Indian history on the basis of dynasties that ruled, it was difficult to talk in terms of modes of production and social formations. The ambitious task that the historian D. D. Kosambi had outlined for Indian historians – to present 'in chronological order of successive changes in the means and relations of production'[11] still remains a query like task.

Hence history has not been primarily about isolated 'facts' or details. It tries to select, arrange, analyse and explain them through narratives which are diverse, change- seeking, often mutually conflicting. Relativistic doubts and questionings do not stand entirely irrelevant here. A bit of information about the past becomes a historical 'fact' only within a particular narrative, which would be based on a set of hypotheses or frame of analysis. In a sense, then, it is 'constituted' by the latter. Of course, it depends largely on the historian how he encashes his knowledge on the information towards presenting it into a flair–led historical asset devoid of biases and prejudices.

This three phase division got entrenched in the school and university education so much so that it still continues to this day. Part of the reason was that it neatly matched the three year school and undergraduate courses in history. So the threefold division was retained with a little shifting of the dates to give it a veneer of secularism. Thus instead of commencing the medieval period with the establishment of Muslim rule in 1190, the 'cut-off point' was shifted to the death of Harshavardhana around circa 650 CE.[12] This interestingly was supposed to mark the end of large empires and the beginning of feudalism.

Besides nurturing popular notions of history through the teaching of history in schools and colleges it has also had implication for production of historical knowledge. It is generally presumed that one understands ancient history with the help of archaeology, epigraphy and Sanskrit texts; medieval period is studied mainly with the help of Persian chronicles and documents and finally the modern period is understood by a study of English documents preserved in British and Indian archives. Thus even in the so-called progressive university departments a segment called 'early medieval history' has been created and that has remained within the jurisdiction of the ancient history sections. This essentially covers the period prior to the establishment of the Sultanate. The ostensible reason for this is that the sources for this period continue to be in Sanskrit and epigraphs constitute the bulk of primary sources. This is of course highly questionable as we start getting large volumes of epigraphs in regional languages and literature in non- Sanskrit languages including Persian and Arabic forms the bulk of our sources for this period. Using language as a demarcator tends to promote a communal divide among researchers. Despite notable exceptions the general trend observed has been the Hindu as well as Muslim students take up ancient history and medieval period for study presumably because they are assessed to have easier access to Sanskrit or Persian respectively.

Because of such unreasonable and unjustifiable means, methods of study have also got compartmentalised. Thus for generations, historians have failed to ask elementary questions which familiarity with different kinds of sources and sources of different periods would have necessitated. For example, Medievalists have seldom looked at Navyanyaya texts which proclaim a paradigm shift in Brahmanic philosophy; nor have they asked the question as to what happened to the Brahmin land grantees who so predominate the historiography of the 'early medieval' period. Modern historians with the notable exception of non-Indian scholars have treated the zamindars as creatures of the Permanent Settlement and have seldom raised the question as to what happened to the zamindars who happened to be proved so crucial to the Mughal statecraft. The breaks in Indian social history are perhaps not as sharp as they would seem from such apartheid studies – they are more historiographical breaks than perhaps real. Here also the issue of periodisation raises volumes of queries.

Of course, archaeology is not even remotely considered a possible source for Medieval or Modern history. A major exception of course is the work on Vijayanagar which incidentally is treated as a part of the Ancient period because of its Hindu ruling elite.[13] In another exception Iqtidar Alam Khan has used field survey of Mughal structures to reconstruct the history of *sarais* and roads and bridges and also indigo technologies. However, the official department of Archaeology has little to show for Medieval Archaeology. In fact, most departments dealing with Archaeology in the Universities are called 'department of Ancient History and Archaeology' as if Archaeology has got relevance only with Ancient history and not with other branches following it. Too much of compartmentalisation delinks the process of continuity in history and hence irks the simple notion of historical lessons putting the crux into ambiguity. This is where we probably go wrong and fail to assign history a definite direction in its aspect of getting classified.

While it is increasingly becoming clear that such division of Indian history is impeding historical research, departments have tenaciously stuck to the older modes more out of concern for petty patronage purposes than any lofty consideration. Today more than ever it has become imperative to break the shackles the threefold division has imposed on the structure of the university departments and consequently upon historical research and the teaching of history at the popular level. Intra and inter-disciplinary approaches to the study of history are in the offing.

To see history and time valid and valuable, past is periodised or divided into different units of time variously called eras, epochs or periods. They serve as important conceptual tools to grasp and comprehend the vast temporal stretch of human history. However, periodising history is not a simple task. First, there are conceptual difficulties in abstraction and generalisation. The problem hinges around the question of locating indicators or variables that determine change in history, which also help draw a dividing line between eras and thus demarcate one historical period from another. Here it does not seem out of place to recall M. Morony's note of caution to historians, who maintains that the apparent cultural and institutional inertia that is generally taken to be continuity in history, is nothing but a slow and gradual change.[14]

Secondly, the whole process of periodisation has been politicised.[15] At times, the criterion of periodising history might be consciously or unconsciously politically driven. So the construction of a historical period may reflect the hidden prejudices of its formulators. Since historical periods are generally taken for granted, their informal citing becomes a source of encouraging the biases and prejudices. Hence historians should critically and over-critically be judgemental before putting his words in a document to be referred for posterity. We do believe that historians are not out of society and polity. They tend to get enormously impacted by the ongoing socio-political trends while writing history. Perceptions apart, reasonables should form the inner-most chore of the historical deliverance. Historical facts never should enter the ambit of jurisprudence. They should be reasonably left safe at the hands of the readers to be felt safe to take up their study and research for again a safe delivery.

Thirdly, since the periodisation of history is firmly rooted in academic traditions, it restricts historical thinking and imagination. One also finds oneself confined in its conceptual barrier. As generally people tend to think within their given categories, it becomes difficult to transcend the conceptual categories of periodisation and go beyond them. Referring to this 'rigidifying power of periodisation', William Green has rightly put: "Once firmly drawn and widely accepted, period frontiers can become intellectual straitjackets that profoundly affect our habits of mind—the way we retain images, make associations and perceive the beginning, middle and ending of things." [16]

Lastly, as seen, some of the notions on historical periodisation have gone bulky. With the change of time, a thick layer of interpretation has got sedimented on them, making them heavy, biased and politically-backed. Their non-academic use has put the scholars in a fix for their scholarly interpretation as one of the sources of historiography. They have lost their neutrality as concepts. Presently, periodisation of history as units of historical studies has gained varied connotations, the most common being the tripartite scheme of Ancient-Medieval-Modern periods in consonance with the dominant standard periodisation of European history since the eighteenth century going by the nomenclature, the Ancient, Medieval and Modern, followed by the colonial scheme of partition, putting 'Yes' to it, of the history of the colonised regions in Africa and Asia, including India.

At the turn of the twentieth century the Ancient-Medieval-Modern scheme of division of Indian history was adopted in South Asia, which replaced the Orientalists' triadic formulation of Hindu, Muslim and British periods of Indian history. The term 'Medieval India' went by the name 'Muslim India', as interpreted by the Orientalists. In fact, the so-called Hindu, Muslim and British periods roughly correspond with the Ancient, Medieval and Modern eras of Indian history. In contemporary South Asian historiographical traditions, the latter chronological constructs are now commonly used as convenient labels. The Medieval period in Indian history, as in European history, is often referred to as the 'Middle Ages'. It is understood as a post-classical age denoting a radical shift from Ancient or classical period. Moreover, there seems to be an inherent bias in it, as it implies decline and degeneration in Medieval times as opposed to the splendour and glory of the Ancient past.

Even if such tripartite division has gained much currency, no consensus among historians as to what constitutes 'Medieval India' is yet to be reached at. As for the Ancient India, almost all historians begin it with an account of the pre-historic times followed by the Aryan invasion and the Vedic age, but the problem arises where to bring ancient India to a close and commence the Medieval period of Indian history. The indicators or variables determining the transition from the Ancient to the Medieval in Indian context have been a subject of 'controversial variables' among historians, who have brought rigidified different chronological references arguing for different chronological era for such division.

Some historians say, Ancient period continued till sixth/ seventh century A.D.,[17] while some others opine it continuing till the close of the twelfth or the beginning of the thirteenth century.[18] According to the former scheme, the chronological reference points seem to be the Arab invasion of Sindh and Gujarat in 711 A.D., whereas the latter corresponds to the establishment of Delhi Sultanate in Northern India in the wake of Sultan Muhammad Ghori's death in 1206 A.D. Being reinforced by textbooks, the latter scheme is more commonly accepted among the students of history. Quite apropos to note here that historians accepting the first decade of thirteenth century as a transition from Ancient to Medieval have not overlooked the historical significance the Arab invasion of Sindh and Gujarat has borne. It is for this reason that ancient India has further been sub-divided by some historians into two periods; first up to 711 A.D. and second from 712 to 1206 A. D.[19]

The most accepted common notion stands that Medieval India starts from the establishment of Muslim rule in India. The origin of this notion goes back to the Medieval historians such as Mulla Abdul Qadir Badauni (C. 1540 - 1615),[20] an Indo-Persian historian and translator living in the Mughal Empire and the author of *Muntakhab al-Tawarikh* (Selection of Chronicles), composed in three volumes in 1595 A.D. to whom the Muslim conquest of India served as a convenient dividing line for historical periodisation.[21] Again there is no commonality as to when the actual commencement of the Muslim rule in India did begin. Badauni for instance, begins his account with the conquest of north-western regions of India by Sultan Mahmud of Ghazni which resulted in the establishment of Muslim political power in regions like the Punjab, Multan and parts of Sindh, whereas most of the contemporary historians have taken the establishment of Delhi Sultanate in northern India in the first decade of the thirteenth century as the dividing line.

Here is another interpretation put by Harbans Mukhia. He goes to say that it was under the influence of the Arab historiographical traditions that most of the Muslim historians of medieval India had employed the '*jahiliyya*-Islam dichotomy' (*jahiliyya* being the Islamic term for the pre-Islamic age of ignorance and Islam for truth) for periodisation of Indian history.[22] It may be true for the historians of Medieval India, Badauni as an example, for whom the conquest of north-western regions of India by Sultan Mahmud of Ghazni was primarily a religious phenomenon, as it facilitated the spread of Islam in the conquered regions. But needless to mention here that the contemporary historians who accept the establishment of Delhi Sultanate as a dividing line between Ancient and Medieval India, have referred to it as a historical concurrence, prioritising political significance rather than religious.

Most of the historians, with few exceptions, accept the medieval period of Indian history stretching from twelfth to the eighteenth century A.D. They have gone exploring some variables proved to be indicators for distinguishing the medieval era from that of the ancient. Regarding this historiographical abstraction of period frontier of Medieval India, J. S. Grewal observes that it is based on a few assumptions including the hegemony of Muslim political power in Indian politics, the presence of two distinct communities- the Hindus and the Muslims in India and interaction between the Hindu and Muslim societies in religious, social, cultural and political spheres. Moreover, the intellectual and institutional differences between the age to which these contemporary historians belonged and the times about which they were writing also conditioned their conceptualisation of Medieval India.[23]

With regard to the first characteristic of medieval India, i.e., the hegemony of Muslim political power, it can be said to be true for the northern part of India. In its first phase, in addition to the Sultanate, there existed powerful rival kingdoms of Chola in south India and Chalukya, Vijayanagar and Bahmani Kingdoms in Deccan. Excluding the Bahmani Kingdom, rest of them were ruled by Hindu rajas. Moreover, there existed other kingdoms in Jaunpur, Malwa and Gujarat, but they were not as powerful as other kingdoms. However, the chronological label of medievalism is not only used in relation to the Sultanate in north India alone, it is also used for the Cholas in south India and the Chalukyas in Deccan as well.[24] As for the question of Muslim political hegemony, it was under Sultan Ala ud-din Khalji (r. 1296-1316) that the Muslim rule expanded to the south in Deccan,[25] though dispelled. Later, the Mughal Empire enjoyed considerable territorial stretch and under Aurangzeb the vast areas of Deccan were annexed enveloping them under the Muslim rule. In short, the hegemony of the Muslim political power in entire India was neither absolute and complete, nor consistent and linear throughout the Medieval period. Regarding the second characteristic of Medieval India, interaction between the Hindu and Muslim societies in various spheres did occur, but the phenomenon of the Hindu and Muslim communities existing side by side reflecting communal harmony and tolerance has also been a subject of controversy among historians.

Nihar Ranjan Ray goes to include emergence of regional dynasties, transition from a money economy to a natural economy, crystallisation of regional characteristics in language and literature, proliferation of sects and sub-sects in religious sphere, and development of regional schools in art within the other characteristics of Indian 'medievalism'.[26] B. D. Chattopadhyaya criticises Ray in this aspect and says that Ray draws his parallels of interpretation from European history and his explanation is based on the Indian feudalism model.[27] Such parallel in respect of the Medieval period of Indian history does not exactly correspond with the Middle Ages of Europe. Of course, the debate on the transition from Ancient to Medieval period has been closely associated to the issue of the rise of feudalism. We find numerous advocates as well as critics among Indologists for Indian feudalism.[28] In fact, feudalism originated in Western Europe in post-classical age or Medieval times and for this reason, the terms 'feudal' and 'Medieval' have mistakenly gained currency as inter-receptive terms in non-academic dealings. What the scholars have come to construe is that the European set of feudalism as an economic, social and political order was largely different from that of the Indian society. Hence usage of the term 'feudal' in non-European contexts has put the issue of periodisation almost in a fix. Since the conceptualisation of periodisation in Indian history is largely Euro-centric, 'Indian feudalism' has mistakenly been interpreted as an explanatory model to denote the transition from the Ancient to the Medieval era.

Medieval era, like ancient period, has too been sub-divided into eras. According to Nihar Ranjan Ray, for example, Medieval India stretches from the seventh to eightienth centuries, with three sub-periods: (i) seventh to twelfth centuries; (ii) twelfth to the first quarter of the sixteenth centuries; and (iii) first quarter of the sixteenth to the close of the eighteenth centuries.[29] Nonetheless, the most common sub-divisions are the early and later Medieval periods. Again, there are differing views of historians regarding their chronological span. The period from 1206-1526 was assigned the label of early Medieval India by Indian History Congress.[30] Early Medieval is used for referring to the period stretching from the Arab invasion of Sindh and Gujarat in early eighth century to the decline of Delhi Sultanate by Professor Mohammad Habib.[31] B. D. Chattopadhyaya, however, treats the span of six hundred years (from seventh to thirteenth centuries A.D.) as early Medieval India.[32] Andre' Wink includes seventh to eleventh centuries in early Medieval India.[33] As for the later Medieval era, those who treat pre-Sultanate times as early Medieval period, refer to the Sultanate of Delhi as later Medieval India, but others include Mughal Dynasty in later Medieval period. For instance, A. B. Pandey goes to cover the era from the establishment of Mughal rule in India with the advent of Babur in 1526 to eighteenth century A.D.[34]

The authenticity of using the very term 'Medieval' has too been questioned by historians. While Timothy Reuter, in his article 'Medieval: Another Tyrannous Construct?' argues that the term 'Medieval' is too conventionalised to be of much use for the purpose of dialogue between medievalists of different geographical locales, since "it does not clearly define either a social formation or a stage of development".[35] Chattopadhyaya, in his monument, *The Making of Early Medieval India*, contends that "continuing with the term 'early Medieval', rather than using terms such as 'late Hindu' or 'late classical', has an advantage. This term goes beyond the narrowly political and cultural dimensions of history and further, it clearly projects continuities in the operation of major societal processes well into later phases of Indian history."[36]

So one finds historians putting their views on diverse canvas, some advocating dispel of the use of the term 'Medieval' and others suggesting its use on concessional grounds. Such dichotomy-narratives have naturally invited biases into the orbit of historical analysis on the issue discussed above.

If we take eighteenth century the closing date of Medieval India, we have also to take it as the beginning of Modern India since this century witnessed the rise and growth of the British power in India. For historians, from eighteenth century onwards begins the Modern era, which continues to date. For instance, Stanley Lane-Poole has brought Medieval India to a close in eighteenth century, with the British victory and defeat of the Mughals in the Battle of Buxar in 1764 as a dividing line, indicating the fall of the Mughal Empire and the Hindu Revival in India.[37] In this case, Battle of Buxar has been taken as a chronological reference point, as it signified the first major step towards the British paramountcy over Indian political system.

It seems evident from the above discussion that with the passage of time the term 'Medieval' kept wide varieties of its meanings abreast, making it more bulky and biased, losing its neutrality as a concept. The term, far from its usage as a concept in historical studies, has come to denote derogatory connotations in everyday speech and language. References to the Medieval psyche of Talibans, Medieval mindset of feudal lords and Medieval Islam[38] are common examples in point which go to show a great line of contradictions on the use of the term 'Medieval' as an era in the periodisation of Indian history.

The periodisation of Indian history into three periods, i.e., Hindu, Muslim and British can be traced back to the succinct opinion made by the eminent Scottish philosopher, historian and economist James Mill (1773-1836) in his work *History of British India*, 3 vol. (1817). Out and out a Utilitarian, Mill got associated with the India House for a period of 17 years (1819-1836) and rose gradually through the ranks until he was appointed head of the examiner's office in 1830. The *History,* his major literary achievement, was the first full historical treatment of the British conquest of India whereby he was scornful of the British administration in India. However, his severe Utilitarian analysis of Indian civilisation (without even visiting India) leading to the construction of an image of the subcontinent as perpetually backward and undeveloped among European readers did not go unbiased.

The kind of classification Mill made was based on the nationality or religions of the ruling class which rendered a communal tinge to the narratives of Indian history.[39] This seems to have been, as if, forcibly done jeopardising the inherent flow of structuralism in history. However, such periodisation was followed by the historians until some historians questioned its validity and significance. At present mostly the scholars use the nomenclature, Ancient, Medieval and Modern in place of Hindu, Muslim and British. But there is no consensus among the historians on the exact terminal date of these periods. Generally, it is construed that the Ancient begins with the Harappan Culture from C.2500 B.C. and ends with C.1000 A.D. or 1200 A.D. The advent of Muslims as the most dominating political power in India is accepted as the end of the Ancient and the beginning of the Medieval period. The year 1757 is generally taken as the end of the Medieval and the beginning of the Modern period. The Battle of Plassey was definitely a turning point in Indian history since it offered the British a strong footage to hegemonise their political power over Bengal, a strong state of the eighteenth century India.[40]

Even if we accept in a broader spectrum these terminating dates for the division of the Ancient, Medieval and Modern periods of Indian history, it can hardly be applied fully to the regional history, specifically to the history of the Deccan and South India, Eastern, north-eastern and frontier India. Whatever way the periodisation in Indian history has been made, it is mainly based on the history of the Northern India with its geographical thrust on the Gangetic valley. Looking at the structure of history of the whole of India such division is hardly to be made acceptable, because there is no uniform and common date for the establishment of Muslim rule in India. The arrival of Muslims in different parts varies in time which raises question of validity of transition of regional history from Ancient to Medieval. Similarly, the foundation of British rule which is taken as the beginning of the Modern period varies at different regions of India. This naturally has asked the historians to believe in a different period of beginning of the Modern history.

Given the kind of discussions held above North East India has got a peculiar scenario. It could succeed in getting itself as a separate unit but in the process, was seen 'different' from the rest of India and a classic periphery. The students of North East India are taught that it was an independent political unit in the pre-colonial period. It had maintained its 'splendid isolation'.[41] It could no way be discussed what was splendid about this isolation, nor be explained that the independence of Assam in the pre-colonial times was not an isolated phenomenon. The entire Medieval world including India was characterised by such regionalism where autonomous units thrived. Nation and nation-states are only a modern phenomenon. Multiplicity of regional kingdoms and feudal chiefdoms, fragmentation of empire, appearance and disappearance of regional powers, regionalism and insularity in vision and political action are characteristics of Medieval time. It is a significant failure of the regional historiography to highlight that Assam could not have been an exception to these medieval characteristics. A scholar discovers a strange insularity in the historiography of North East India in the sense that it never tried to view its history against the background of developments in India as a whole.[42] He also found that there is a discernible lack of interest or information about North East India outside north east.[43]

To begin with Ancient India and the problem of periodisation in Indian history, the name of Bhaskarvarman does not seem to be an alien one if Ancient history of India is dealt specifically in the post-Gupta period. He was the one who not only won the alliance of the King Harsha, carried his arms into Bengal increasing the power and prestige of the kingdom of Kamarupa to an extent never dreamt before[44], but also stood out as a patron of letters. He figures prominently in Huen Tsang's Account as well as in the *Harshacharita*. Sir Edward Gait writes, "Bhaskarvarman has left behind him a name uttered in the same breath with the noblest monarchs of India."[45] And yet, he does not find so much a place as he deserves as put by O. P. Kejariwal[46] in Romila Thapar's *History of India.* Seldom does it find an independent mention, all the time being clubbed either with Bengal, Nepal, or Odisha[47] or treated as a mere trade route between Burma and the rest of India.[48]

On the question of periodisation the need for re-examining the stereotyped division of Indian history into Ancient, Medieval and Modern, coinciding with the Hindu, Muslim and British periods has been a recurring theme in Dr Thapar's aspects of Indian history and needs revision. There are also some suggestions on the lines on which this could be done. To any scholar conversant with the history of the north-east, this stereotyped division of Indian history into the Hindu and Muslim periods on the basis of the establishment of the Muslim rule is irrelevant to this region. This area successfully withstood the onslaught of the Muslim invaders down to the time of Aurangzeb. Again as put by Amalendu Guha, "this kind of neat periodisation breaks down the moment the historian enters the preliterate parts of the region".[49] These factors could have provided significant sign-posts to a historian, but they do not find any mention in any of the books dealing with the subject. The reason can only be that the veil of historical unawareness about the north-east continues to prevail on the general historian of India.

Given the kind of discussion held above, if the Medieval period marks the beginning of the conquest of the Muslim invaders, then it must be stated that there was no Medieval period in Assam. Mohammed Bakhtiyar, Ghiyas-ud-din and Tughril Khan and other Muslim rulers who tried to subjugate this area failed time and again. Their trite failure to get hold of this region on their spree of conquest-attempts does not necessarily disprove the narratives that this region did not have the criteria of being included within the greater narratives for determining the former to be a part of the period as we discuss here. If subjugation of territories followed by conquests is taken a positive stance for the kind of proposition we used to suggest, the repulsions and resistances shown at the local levels towards the same conquest-attempts are not less historical conjectures to be included as under 'bigger connotation' of the dialectics of history. This is neither less heroic, less championing, less valiant and less entrepreneuring nor anti-relevant and anti-inspirational. This in itself should be treated as a significant aspect in Indian history. Moreover, the Ahom King Rudra Singha's attempt at forging an army by inviting the Kachari and the Jaintia kings to join him in his mission of attacking the powerful Mughals is an episode showing intrepidity and hegemony of the ruler at the regional level. This should have featured in every book on Indian history and unfortunately does not find a place in any.

If the non-inclusion of many of the aspects of Ancient and Medieval history of the north-east in the general histories of India is sought to be explained away by the paucity of materials available, the same does not hold good for the Modern period. After the East India Company established its hold on most of the areas of this region, there was a volume of reports and studies on various aspects including the tribes of this region. Thus besides the valuable accounts of John Wade, Buchanon Hamilton and David Scott, also available are the reports of Francis Jenkins, Richard Pemberton and William Robinson. Sir Edward Gait's *History of Assam* and 'Report on the Progress of Historical Research in Assam' (1897) are milestones in the study of the history of this region. Even the study of the different tribes of the north east by E. Stach, Charles Lyall, R. S. Endle, Gurdon, Playfair, W. Shaw, J. Shakespeare, T. C. Hudson, W. C. Smith, J. P. Mills and J. H. Hutton was outstandingly undertaken and they in themselves prove to be important edifice for the study of the history of the north east.

It can perhaps still be argued that little or no material is available on this region which has got an all-India bearing and hence this region has been overlooked in general histories of India. This may be correct to an extent, but what is more obvious is that this region has not so far been an inherent part of the historical consciousness of India. If it were, then there should have been discussions on why such an event or development taking place in the rest of India had little or no impact in this region. Now with the emphasis of historical writing shifting from dynastic and political history to the history of the people, the omission of this region seems all the more glaring. Certainly, the people here did not live forever in a preliterate and pre-historical stage. Their social institutions and economic conditions changed and developed during the period when the rest of India underwent transformations. The two streams may not have been parallel, but in any case, this development has never been uniform all over the country over the same period of time. For a proper perspective, therefore, histories of India must take into account the dynamics this region has undergone and if they are found different from those occurring in other parts of India, then the historian must take the baton to explain the reasons why they go different.

As for the modern period it is also pointed out that the British had no intention of conquering the tribes of the north east as it would not gain much economically by such a conquest[50] as these hills were "not a land of flowing milk and honey, no glittering outcrops to raise thoughts of mineral wealth, no telling indications of reservoirs of endless oil."[51] It is overlooked that imperialism was its own justification. 'Economic' motive did not remain necessarily all the time a potential factor for a 'conquest'. These few lines of Edward Gait in the context of extending the British rule over the Nagas quite substantiate the proposition. Here they go- "At last in 1866, it was resolved to take possession of the Angami country and reclaim its inhabitants from savagery...The object in view was to protect the low land from the incursions of the Nagas. It was not desired to extend British rule into the interior, but when a footing in the hills had once been obtained; further territorial expansion became almost inevitable."[52]

Let us discuss on another version holding quite apropos to this. B. C. Allen puts- "It should be first premised that for the annexation of their territory, the Nagas themselves are responsible. The cost of administration of the district is out of all proportion to the revenue that is obtained, and we only occupied the hills after a bitter experience, extending over many years, which clearly showed that annexation was the only way of preventing raids upon our villages...it was impossible for any civilised power to acquiesce in the perpetual harrying of its border folk."[53]

The naivete of the regional historiography of north east India is reflected in the contention that the annexation of the Naga or Mizo hills was a historical accident. It only carries forward the argument of colonialism itself that the British had no intentions of conquering these hills which stood not only devoid of any natural resources but proved to be a liability to the British; it is only the 'barbarism' of the tribes which forced their conquest. Colonialism had not only conquered India, it had conquered Indian mind too. While the mainstream historiography had been able to by and large decolonize it, the regional counterpart could not yet do so. The absence of motives, pre-plans, strategies, benefits in the conquest of Naga-Mizo hills was seen as a legitimisation of colonial arguments. It not only refuses to acknowledge the reality of 'conquests' itself but undermines the nature and strength of imperialism itself. The story of the conquest of the Naga-Mizo tribes lasting about a century which imperialism describes as "one long sickening story of open insults and defiance, bold outrages and cold blooded murders on the one side and long-suffering forbearance, forgiveness, concession and unlooked favours on the other"[54] is a long drawn story to testify the claim of the colonial historiography.

The fact that the hills were occupied and devastated was overlooked and the emphasis was on whether the British had any motive for the conquest or not. Had the British ever publicized or professed its intention of conquests at any stage of their conquering spree in India? Similarly, the imperialist concepts like non-intervention, non-interference and non-regularisations were uncritically accepted without inquiring into their epistemological background or imperial legitimisation.[55] It is said that the Inner Line Regulation was a device to safeguard the identity of the tribals whereas tribal identity was never discussed in the Inner Line Regulation document.[56] The primary motive, as shown later, was to restrict the European planters from occupying tribal lands for the purpose of tea-plantation and secondly stop Indian merchants from encroaching on the trades that were the monopoly of the tribals like collection of rubber, ivory, tribal salt and other forest products.[57] These studies themselves show that despite the claims of non-interference, 'interference' had been a tested truth for the British on their deal with the tribes of the north east.

It is a fact that chronology is the only tool by which periodisation of regional history can be validated. But unfortunately history of Arunachal Pradesh does not have a chronological sequence of historical process and development. History of Arunachal presents altogether a different scenario which does not conform to aforesaid characteristics of periodisation. A good work of history starts with the collection of relevant historical materials from different sources. This constitutes the first step of historical research, the second stage being the analytical operation of materials. While the systematic arrangement of raw materials is considered the third step of the same, the final construction by the synthetic operation and exposition is taken as the last one in historical research. Having considered briefly the process of conducting historical research, the historian has to seek, select, analyze, compare, construct, deconstruct, reconstruct and review the past from the varied sources.[5]

To conduct historical research in Arunachal Pradesh is very difficult since materials, written or unwritten, relating to its history other than some oral literature and certain historical ruins lying in the foot hills of the territory are practically not available. Initially upto 1865, the scholars knew of only three ruins namely, Bhalukpong in the West Kameng District and Tamreswari temple and Bhismaknagar in the Lohit District. But as a result of subsequent explorations and excavations a good number of other such ruins dating approximately from the early Christian era have been brought to light.[59] Hence, it will not be exaggeration to say that the history of Arunachal Pradesh is mixed with legends, folklores and traditional accounts. The history of Arunachal Pradesh has so far remained hidden. There is a dearth of historical materials of the socio-political history of the source materials pertaining to the socio-political conditions of the state.[60]

So far as the early history of the people of Arunachal in Ancient India is concerned it is scanty and sparse having no chronology at all compared to other regional early history while its immediate border state Assam then named Kamarupa or Pragjyotisha possesses a strong early history in Ancient India with sources and chronology with which Arunachal had accessibility excepting certain stray references of mythological narratives and archaeological remains[61] of present day Arunachal. Tamo Mibang rightly points out, "Our knowledge about the early history of the people of Arunachal Pradesh is extremely vague and no connected account of the events that took place in later times is available. So it is not at all possible to trace the original home, the routes of immigration and dates of settlement of our myriad tribes and consequently we are bound to rely on local traditions, legends and some scanty information of the Ahom and British record".[62] Even no radio carbon dating has so far been made possible in the region to ascertain the age of the palaeolithic sites deciphered in some of the regions which is discussed in the later lines.

W. Robinson contextually observes, "It seems almost vain to attempt to lift up the dark veil which conceals the origin of the tribes to trace back their history, or to gain any information of the various revolutions by which they have been influenced, these subjects belong to times and circumstances which are beyond the limit of certain knowledge. It would be most cautious and perhaps the most philosophical course to abstain from any conjecture relating to their origin or from any attempt to penetrate into the nature of causes of which even the most distant results are but partially known to us."[63]

Despite the constraints of availability of source materials and topographical hazards in Arunachal Pradesh, scholars and archaeologists dared to delve into the region to decipher the archaeological remains and historical monuments so as to ascertain the presence of some symbols of ancient history of Arunachal. Some of such historical evidences could here be discussed as relevant supplements to the topic under observation. A survey of the prehistoric findings in Arunachal reveals that most of them are exploratory in nature without any stratigraphic time scale under geochronology. Only Parsi-Parlo site of the Damin circle in the Lower Subansiri district where some Neolithic tools could be excavated by A. A. Ashraf during 1982-83 gives us an idea of cultural development from a Ceramic Neolithic to Ferrolithic stage.[64] Ceramic objects are almost as old as the human race. However, various Palaeolithic tools from Dapbhum in the Lohit district discovered by B. P. Bopardikar in 1969-70;[65] single specimen from Pagam in Lower Subansiri area excavated by A. A. Ashraf [66] along with evidence of fossil in Arunachal indicate the existence of Lower Palaeolithic culture here. The discovery of a vertebrate fossil by the geologists in 1974-75 from the Upper Tertiary rocks of Ramghat area in the Lower Subansiri district of Arunachal Pradesh proves to be quite significant in so far as it indicates the continuation of Siwaliks to the Eastern Himalayas or Arunachal Siwaliks. The Upper Tertiary horizon of Arunachal now seems to have been inhabited by Hominids and Palaeolithic men.[67] Their proximity, ecological identity and similarity of remains suggest that they belonged to the same ethnic tribes, who were also responsible for the contemporary cultures of North East India, Burma, South China and South-East Asian Countries.

A few Accounts of the Greek travellers to India in early Christian era refer to the land and people of Arunachal Pradesh. Pliny, in his book *Natural History* (first century A.D.) gives an account of the people of the frontier Himalayan regions which gives us an indication that these people were the Tibeto-Burman tribes of northern Assam. Pliny refers to the people like the Syrites, Mandai, the Ornulae, Coribae and the Abali; the Ornulae and Abali being identified as the Akas of West Kameng district and Abors (Adis) of East Siang district of Arunachal Pradesh respectively. The Chinese traveller Yuan Chwang (seventh century A.D.) is said to have mentioned the Adi people of Arunachal, as mentioned by Edward Gait in his book, *A History of Assam.*[68]

Sculptural remains found mainly consisting of religious icons are numerous. Living and old monuments of Buddhist, Hindu and tribal religion are repositories of religious icons, fetishes and human and animal figures connected with different forms of religious worship. Monasteries, chapels and private households are found to have preserved stone, metal and clay images for worship. Tawang, Zemithang, Kalaktang, Dirang, Rupa, Shergaon and other places of Tawang and West Kameng districts; Mechuka, Tuting, Gelling, Mankhota and other sites of the upper parts of the West Siang and Dibang Valley districts are full of Buddhist gompas, monasteries and chortens (Stupas) belonging to the different sects of Vajrayana Buddhism, constructed during different periods. Images preserved in monasteries and gompas traditionally ascribe to the eleventh-twelfth centuries A.D. or still earlier times.[69]

Beautiful icons of Hindu deities discovered from the temple at Malinithan of the West Siang district are variously datable to different periods between the tenth and fourteenth centuries.[70] The *Kalikapurana* states that there was a pithasthana east of Kamakhya and Malinithan is identified with that pithasthana. Malinithan, once a gigantic temple was built of stones as found in other temples of India particularly those in Orissa of ninth to twelfth centuries A.D. The widely scattered archaeological remains at different places in Arunachal Pradesh bear testimony to its rich cultural heritage. Excavations at Bhismaknagar in Dibang Valley which was once a strong hold of Chutiyas between twelfth to sixteenth centuries A.D. have revealed the high standard of civilisation that once prevailed in the state in ancient times.[71] Forts of Bhalukpong in the West Kameng district and Itanagar in the Papum Pare district have so far yielded a few stone terracotta and metal figurines which demonstrate various phases of cultural movements in Arunachal. Migration of different ethnic groups, their admixture and cultural contact with the world beyond its present geographical limits are vividly recorded amidst the sculptural treasures as well as in other material remains and literature.

Inscriptions found within the boundaries of present Arunachal Pradesh so far known do not go beyond fourteenth century A.D. Some of the epigraphic documents bear specific dates while in case of others paleography and circumstantial evidence help to ascertain their time and place of origin. The earliest datable inscription is found from the Tamresvari Temple in the Lohit district written in Sanskrit language and Assamese-Bengali script of the fifteenth century A.D. which throws some light on the political, religious and cultural history of the period.[72] Subid Chatterjee writes, "It would seem from all evidences that from around the first millennium B.C. these Mongoloid speakers of the Tibeto-Burman languages were in a dominant position in the Himalayan region of North Eastern India, including Arunachal Pradesh. Available indications from contiguous regions would suggest their co-existence for quite some time till through the process of miscegenation and absorption by waves after waves of the newcomer's vestiges of the independent existence of the earlier settlers were largely obliterated."[73]

All these discussions go to suggest that there was no fixed chronological date which could be put into the framework of ancient Indian history of Arunachal Pradesh compared to the historical process taking place in northern India according to which periodisation is made. Arunachal accounts for a varied datable chronology deciphered so far spanning over from palaeolithic culture to fifteenth century A.D. which itself shows both Ancient and Medieval historical occurrences of Arunachal Pradesh within it. There is no definite and significant historical phenomenon occurring in the region which could be taken as a yardstick to differentiate medieval from that of ancient as is the justification in case of periodisation of Ancient and Medieval Indian history. If Ancient Indian history begins with the Harappan Culture from 2500 B.C. and ends up with 1000 A.D. or 1200 A.D. and the Medieval Indian history with the advent of the Muslims as the dominating political power, no such evidences are available so far in Arunachal Pradesh in order to ascertain their contemporaneity with Indian.

If we take Assam as a feeder region with which Arunachal Pradesh had larger accessibility, a different kind of historical conjecture emerges in a medieval set-up. Assam comes in contact with the Turko-Afghan rulers of Bengal in the early part of thirteenth century A.D. when the first expedition to Kamarupa (Assam then known) during the period of the Delhi Sultanate led by Muhammed-bin-Bakhtiyar Khalji, the Governor of Bihar under Qutb-ud-din Aibak takes place in 1205 A.D.[74] Even then Assam was not conquered and ruled by the Turko-Afghans during the medieval period of her history. Mention may be made that it was a kingdom by the Tai-Shans popularly known as 'Ahoms' which was founded in Assam during the same period which continued from 1228 A.D. to 1826 A.D. Here, in case of Assam the advent of Muslims does not seem to have played as significant a role as the advent of the Ahoms, in testifying its corroboration to the criterion for periodisation of medieval Indian history. If it is so with Assam, it is far less with Arunachal Pradesh, practically showing nil influence of the Muslims on its history, polity and economy.

The above discussion shows a complete different historical development in Arunachal Pradesh in comparison to the history of Northern India. Scholars have used different parameters to periodise Indian history. Cultural changes in India in the post-Gupta period which marked the end of all India classical period in the sixth or seventh century A.D. are suggested as the starting of medieval period in Indian history.[75] Further, the post-Gupta period in which certain economic factors played a decisive role such as the feudalisation of state-apparatus through land grants, gradual decline of trade, money economy and commodity production, decay of urban centres, rise of local units of production and self-sufficient village economy is taken as a transition-period from Ancient to Medieval Indian history.[76] Techno-economic changes that took place with the foundation of the rule of the Delhi Sultanate with qualitative changes on material aspects of Indian culture by the introduction of Persian wheel, mechanism of the handloom, paper production etc. also are taken as the beginning of the Medieval period in Indian history.[77] Though the religion of the ruler or the ruling class should not be taken as a criterion for periodisation, there is no doubt that the establishment of Islam as the most dominant political power with major administrative changes in the Indian sub-continent in the twelfth-thirteenth century A.D. marked a turning point in Indian history which signifies the end of the Ancient period and beginning of the Medieval one.

Even if we take these parameters, it is difficult to periodise the history of Arunachal Pradesh in the above chronological framework. The political and dynastic history is completely missing from the annals of Arunachal history right from the ancient period to the modern with the absence of kingdoms and their rule except those of the genealogical and migrational myths of the tribes and tribal politics. Hinting on the political history of Arunachal Pradesh, Professor A. C. Talukdar writes, "The process of administrative and constitutional development of Arunachal Pradesh started about a century back when the British extended their administration to certain parts of this territory. Arunachal Pradesh, at that time, presented a picture of a hilly terrain devoid of developed means of communications with a sparse population cut up into numerous isolated tribes or village communities. The people were mostly suspicious of outsiders like any other tribal people. The British had considered the area too backward and unrewarding for extending any civil administration there. The socio-political life of the tribes of the area therefore was untouched by any modernising influence and remained primitive till the early years of our independence".[78]

It is difficult to trace out the relations of the Arunachal tribes with the outside world prior to the sixteenth century A.D. due to want of any authentic record. One of the key factors which regulated these relations was the tough geography of Arunachal and the lack of some of the daily necessities of life in this area, such as salt, iron and clothes etc. To meet these requirements, they had to depend on the plains. Hence they frequently raided the plains and obtained these articles by force. It was the reason why the Ahom ruler Pratap Singha (1603-1641) introduced one 'Posa' system[79] as means of compensation to the tribes to protect the subject of the plains from the raids. The Adi-Ahom relations as early as 1523 and the Nocte-Ahom relations as early as 1536 during the reign of Suhungmung (1497-1539); the Mishmi-Ahom relations as early as the reign of Sutyinpha Nariya Raja (1644-48); the Nyishi-Ahom relations since 1614; the Khampti-Ahom relations since the middle of the eighteenth century; the Singpho-Ahom relations since the reign of Kamaleswar Singha (1795-1811) and the Aka-Ahom relations as early as 1825,[80] all go to show that Arunachal developed some nexus with its neighbouring Assam during the Ahom regime till the British captured Assam in 1826, after the Treaty of Yandaboo.

Hence, politically and culturally Arunachal Pradesh was still in her ancient character upto the early years of India's independence when North India being seen getting transformed from her Ancient to Medieval and from Medieval to Modern. Quite apropos here to ask, can we fix 1523 A.D. (if first ever Ahom-Arunachal relations in the form of Adi-Ahom relations are taken justifiably) as the terminal date for the end of Ancient period and beginning of the Medieval in the history of Arunachal Pradesh? Similarly, it is difficult to characterize the period from 1523 A.D. to the British relations with Arunachal Pradesh in 1825 (if the British nexus with the tribes which began as early as 1825 is taken as the criterion for the end of medieval period and beginning of the modern period) as the Medieval period. No doubt, the Ahom-tribal relations brought some socio-economic and political changes in the then Arunachal, but significant changes are found absent on the basis of which the historians cannot construct vital pillars of historical evidences on medieval history. Here the situation is unlikely of a presence of a strong historical conjecture releasing a safe space to connote specificity to a frame of historiography.

The British is also found to have developed their relations with Arunachal Pradesh in different phases. In the Western side, while they started developing relations with the Akas as early as 1825, with the Sherdukpens as early as 1836 and the Bhutias (termed by the British for Monpas) as early as 1838; in the Central region, their relations began with the Adis as early as 1825, with the Nyishis as early as 1835 and with the Apatanis as early as 1895; and in the Eastern side, they had their relations with Mishmis and Singphos as early as 1825 and with the Khamptis as early as 1830.[81] So, it is difficult to go with an exact date of the beginning of the modern period in Arunachal history if at all the advent of the British to India is taken to be the start-up of a Modern India.

The above evidences prove beyond the doubt the fact that the periodisation of Indian history into the said chronological framework of Ancient, Medieval and Modern cannot strictly be applied to periodise the history of Arunachal Pradesh. It is still a perplexed chapter of the history of the state on which serious attention has to be delved. The facts which are to be put under the framework of Ancient, Medieval and Modern history of Arunachal; from where to where this periodisation is to take place; what should be the accepted terminal dates to fix the beginning and end of such periodisation and what should be the criterion for such periodisation; are some of the important queries which haunt the scholars having interests in the history of Arunachal

Pradesh. Of course, absence of Carbon-14 evidences has posed great challenges before the historians to substantiate the validity of periodisation. A fateful periodisation based upon logical framework, the scholar desires, is expected to go a long way in bringing about scholastic insinuation and enthusiasm among the researchers of the region. That would probably satiate their quest to reach at finality.

Given the type of discussion held above the history of Arunachal Pradesh can justifiably be periodised into four sections, i.e., Pre-history, Proto-history, Pre-British and British. While the archaeological remains from Palaeolithic to Neolithic can be classified as Pre-history, the sculptural remains dealing with religious icons, inscriptions, epigraphic documents and oral sources can certainly be ascribed to Proto-history. Similarly the period from1523 to 1826 (1523 A.D. being the initial year of the Ahom-Arunachal relations in the form of Adi-Ahom relations; and 1826 A.D. being the year of conquest of Assam by the British after the Treaty of Yandaboo) can be put as the Pre-British period. The British relations with the tribes of the state in the post-1826 times till India got independence can also safely be termed as the British period of the history of Arunachal Pradesh.

References

1. The scholar considers history also as a phenomenon like truth since both of them are congruent to each other. A line of difference between the two is that truth takes time to be a part of history.
2. E. H. Carr, *What is History*, London, 1961, p.49.
3. D. A. Suleykin, *Basic Questions of the Periodisation of Ancient Indian History*, Calcutta, 1954. Originally published in Russian from Moscow/Leningrad in 1949.
4. D. D. Kosambi, '*On a Marxist Approach to Indian Chronology*' in Combined Methods in Indology and Other Writings (Ed. B. Chattopadhyaya), New Delhi 2002, pp. 49-50 (originally published in 1951).
5. Romila Thapar, '*Towards the Definition of an Empire: The Mauryan State*' in Romila Thapar, Cultural Pasts, New Delhi 2000, pp. 462-488 (originally published in 1987).

6. B. Subbarao, *The Personality of India*, Baroda, 1958. For a more recent review of the matter, see Bridget and Raymond Allchin, *The Rise of Civilisation in India and Pakistan*, New Delhi 1983 and later editions. Especially, their last chapter entitled 'sub-continental unity and regional diversity'.
7. For a non-Marxist work on the subject see, Harald Tambs-Lyche, *Power, Profit and Poetry. Traditional Society in Kathiawar, Western India*, New Delhi, 1997.
8. For a fruitful study of transmontane and transoceanic interactions see, Irfan Habib's *People's History of India* (three volumes) New Delhi, 2001, 2002 and 2003.
9. *'In broad outline, the Asiatic, ancient, feudal and modern bourgeois modes of production may be designated as epochs marking progress in the economic development of society.'* Karl Marx, *A Contribution to the Critique of Political Economy*, Moscow, 1970, p. 21. Engels built the basis of the concept of primitive communism as preceding the ancient formations in his *Origin of Family, Private Property and the State* (Moscow, 1950). The use of the term primitive communism however came with Stalin's *Dialectical and Historical Materialism.* See *History of the CPSU (B) Short Course* Moscow, 1951, pp. 194-5. Stalin effectively replaced the notion of the Asiatic mode with primitive communism.
10. James Mill, *The History of British India*, New York, 1968.
11. D. D. Kosambi, *The Culture and Civilisation of Ancient India in Historical Outline*, New Delhi 1981, p. 10.
12. This date for the end of the ancient period is used normally in the NCERT history school text books.
13. John M. Fritz, George Michell and D. V. Devraj, Vijayanagara Research Project monographs (5 vols. on various themes), New Delhi various dates around 1995.
14. M. Morony, *Iraq after the Muslim Conquest*, Princeton, 1984, pp. 5, 507, as cited in Aziz Al-Azmeh, "Muslim History: Reflections on Periodisation and Categorisation", *The Medieval History Journal*, Vol. 1, No. 2, (1998), p. 197.
15. Tarif Khalidi has analyzed what one might call the 'politics of periodisation' in Arabic historiography. Tarif Khalidi, "Reflections on Periodisation in Arabic Historiography", *The Medieval History Journal*, Vol. 1, No. 1, (1998), p. 107. For details see pp. 107-24.
16. William A. Green, "Periodisation in European and World History", *Journal of World History*, Vol. 3, No. 1, 1992, p. 14.
17. For instance see R. C. Majumdar (et al.), *An Advanced History of India*, London, 1950.

18. For instance, according to the scheme of periodisation followed in the Indian History Congress, ancient India came to a close in the first decade of 13th century, when Muslim rule was established in Northern India with Delhi as its capital. See *Proceedings of the Indian History Congress*, 13th Session (Nagpur 1950) and 14th Session (Jaipur 1951).
19. *Ibid.*
20. Mulla Abdul Qadir Badauni, *Muntakhab al-Tawarikh*, (ed.), Maulvi Ahmad Ali, Calcutta, 1869.
21. Here the opinion of Lane-Poole seems worth-citing, as he writes that the medieval period "begins when the immemorial systems, rule, and customs of Ancient India were invaded, subdued, and modified by a succession of foreign conquerors who imposed a new rule and introduced an exotic creed, strange languages and a foreign art. These conquerors were Muslims, and with the arrival of the Turks under Mahmud, the iconoclast, at the beginning of the eleventh century, India entered upon her Middle Age." Stanley Lane-Poole, *Mediaeval India Under Muhammedan Rule (A.D. 712-1764),* Lahore, 1997, (first published 1903) p. iii, Preface.
22. Harbans Mukhia, "Medieval India': An Alien Conceptual Hegemony?", *The Medieval History Journal*, Vol. 1, No. 1, (1998), p. 97.
23. J. S. Grewal, *Medieval India: History and Historians*, Amritsar, 1975, p. 134.
24. B. D. Chattopadhyaya, *The Making of Early Medieval India*, New Delhi, 1994, p. 6.
25. The nature of political control in the south is worthy of mention here. The Muslim rule in Deccan was nominal, as the conquered areas were not annexed but only subjugated, and the rulers of small kingdoms were allowed to rule on the condition that they would pay annual tribute to the Sultan. Kishori Saran Lal, *History of the Khaljis A.D. 1290-1320*, Karachi, not dated, pp. 259-60.
26. Nihar Ranjan Ray as cited in Chattopadhyaya, *The Making of Early Medieval India*, p. 9.
27. *Ibid.*
28. See D. D. Kosambi, *An Introduction to the Study of Indian History*, Bombay, 1956, chapters 9 and 10, Harbans Mukhia, "Was there Feudalism in India?", *The Journal of Peasant Studies*, Vol. 8, No. 3., April 1981, pp. 273-310, D. N. Jha, *Feudal Social Formation in Early India*, Delhi, 1987, Brendan O'Leary, *The Asiatic Mode of Production: Oriental Despotism, Historical Materialism and Indian History*, Oxford and Cambridge, (Mass.) 1989, B. D. Chattopadhyaya, "State and Economy in North India: 4th century to 12th century" in Romila Thapar (ed.), *Recent Perspectives of Early Indian History,*

Bombay, 1995, pp. 309-46, and Ram Sharan Sharma, "How Feudal was Indian Feudalism?" in Hermann Kulke (ed.), *State in India 1000-1700*, Delhi, 1995, pp. 48-85.

29. N. R. Ray, "The Medieval Factor in Indian History", General President's Address, *Proceedings of the Indian History Congress*, 29th Session, Patiala, 1967, pp. 1-29.
30. See *Proceedings of the Indian History Congress*, 13th Session, Nagpur, 1950 and 14th Session, Jaipur, 1951.
31. For instance, see K. A. Nizami (ed.), *Politics and Society during the Early Medieval Period: Collected Works of Professor Mohammad Habib,* Delhi, 1974.
32. B. D. Chattopadhyaya, *The Making of Early Medieval India*, *op. cit.*
33. Andre' Wink, *Al-Hind: the Making of the Indo-Islamic World*, Volume I: Early Medieval India and the Expansion of Islam, 7th –11th Centuries, New Delhi, 1999.
34. A. B. Pandey, *Later Medieval India*, Allahabad, 1978.
35. Timothy Reuter, "Medieval: Another Tyrannous Construct?", *The Medieval History Journal*, Vol. 1, No. 1, (1998), p. 25. For a detailed analysis see pp. 25-45.
36. Chattopadhyaya, *The Making of Early Medieval India*, *op. cit.* p. 36.
37. Lane-Poole, *Mediaeval India Under Muhammedan Rule*, *op. cit.*
38. Leila Ahmed, *Women and Gender in Islam*, New Haven and London: Yale University Press, 1992, see the title of Chap. 6, p. 102.
39. For details see, R. Thapar, H. Mukhia and Bipan Chandra, Communalism and Writings of Indian History, PPH, 2nd Edition, New Delhi, 1977.
40. N.R. Ray, Presidential Address to the Indian History Congress, Patiala Session 1967; R. Thapar, *The Past and Prejudice*, Sardar Patel Memorial Lecture, New Delhi, 1975; R. S. Sharma "Problem of Transition from Ancient to Medieval in Indian History", *The Indian Historical Review*, Vol.-I, No. 1, 1974, pp. 1-9; B. N. Mukherjee, "On Periodisation" in S. C. Malik Ed. *Indian Civilisation, The First Phase Problem of a Source Book*, IIAS, Simla 1971, pp.98-99; Barun De, "Encapsulation as an Alternative to the Difficulties of Periodising Indian History", *Ibid*, pp. 83-92.
41. Borrowed from European History, this expression was used in the context of Assam by H. K. Barpujari. But subsequently it was used by a number of authorities, e.g. Subas Chatterjee, *Mizoram under British Rule*, Delhi, 1985, pp. 180-181.
42. O. P. Kejariwal, "The North-East in Indian Historiography: The Need for a Corrective", *Proceedings of the North East India History Association* (hence *PNEIHA*), Pasighat, 1986, pp. 17-24.

43. *Ibid.*
44. R. C. Mazumdar, quoted in Edward Gait, *A History of Assam* (revised and enlarged version), Delhi, 1984, p. 26.
45. *Ibid.*
46. O. P. Kejariwal, *op. cit.*, p. 18.
47. *Ibid.*
48. *Ibid.*
49. Amalendu Guha, "Presidential Address", *PNEIHA*, Dibrugarh, 1981, pp. 1-13.
50. D. R. Syiemlieh, *British Administration in Meghalaya: Policy and Pattern*, New Delhi, 1989, p. 11.
51. Sajal Nag, Aspects of Historiography of North East India, *PNEIHA*, Aizawl, 1996, p. 68.
52. Edward Gait, *History of Assam*, Calcutta, 1905, reprint 1984.
53. B. C. Allen, *Assam District Gazetteer*: Nagaland and Manipur, Shillong, 1905.
54. John Butler, Rough Notes on Angami Nagas, *Journal of Asiatic Society of Bengal*, Vol.44. No.4, 1875, pp. 307-327. Cited in Asoso Yonuo, *The Rising Nagas: A Historical and Political Study*, Delhi, 1974, p. 72.
55. Sajal Nag, *op. cit.*, p. 69.
56. *Ibid.*
57. *Ibid*, p. 70.
58. N. B. Biswas "Historical Research in Arunachal Pradesh: Oral Source and Method, *PNEIHA*, Thirteenth Session, Shillong, 1992, p. 54.
59. L. N. Chakravarty, *Glimpses of the Early History of Arunachal*, Research Department, Government of Arunachal Pradesh, Shillong, 1973 (Reprinted by Annada Printing House, Jorhat, 1995), p. preface.
60. N. B. Biswas, *op. cit*, p. 54.
61. S. L. Baruah, *A Comprehensive History of Assam*, New Delhi, 1977, pp. 85-87.
62. Tamo Mibang, "Origin and Migration of the Tribals of Tirap", *PNEIHA,* Twelfth Session, Jagiroad, 1991, p. 196.
63. W. Robinson, *A Descriptive Account of Assam*, Delhi, 1975, p. 335.
64. D. Pandey and B. K. Tripathy, *A Comprehensive History of Arunachal Pradesh*, Pasighat, 1997, pp. 16-17.
65. Subid Chatterjee, *A Comprehensive History of Arunachal Pradesh.*, Calcutta, 1991, p.4; J. P. Singh and G. Sengupta, *Archaeology of North Eastern India*, New Delhi, 1991, p-69; Also D. Pandey and B. K. Tripathy, *op. cit.*, p. 15.

66. D. Pandey and B. K. Tripathy, *op. cit.*, p. 16-17.
67. Subid Chatterjee, *op. cit.*, pp. 4-5; Also D. Pandey and B. K. Tripathy, *op. cit.*, p. 17.
68. D. Pandey and B. K. Tripathy, *op. cit.*, p. 6-7.
69. Subid Charttejee, *op. cit.*, p. 6.
70. *Ibid*, pp. 6-7.
71. A. K. Paul, *Inspiring Arunachal GK*, Guwahati, 2007, p. 42.
72. Subid Chatterjee, *op. cit.*, pp. 8-9.
73. *Ibid*, p. 120.
74. S. L. Baruah, *op. cit.*, 172.
75. N.R. Ray, *op. cit.*
76. R. S. Sharma, *op. cit.*
77. Irfan Habib, Presidential Address to the Medieval Section of the Indian History Congress, Banaras Session, 1969.
78. A. C. Talukdar, "Political Evolution of Arunachal Pradesh" in S. Dutta (ed) *Studies in the History, Economy and Culture of Arunachal Pradesh*, Itanagar, 1998, pp. 221-222.
79. The term 'Posa' literally means a collection of subscription for a common purpose. It was the practice of collecting forcible exactions from the low lying villages, of the plains, adjacent to the hills, by the tribes of Arunachal Pradesh since the Ahom days. The British commuted this claim of posa into money payment. Details on Posa refer to B. N. Jha, "Politics of Posa: A Case Study of Pre and Post Independence Scenario in Arunachal Pradesh and Assam", *Proceedings of the Indian History Congress*. 57th Session, Madras University, 1996, pp.446-458.
80. D. Pandey and B. K. Tripathy, *op. cit.*, pp. 238-252; Also Laxmi Devi, *Ahom-Tribal Relations*, Calcutta, 1968 (2nd Edn. 1992), pp. 197-248.
81. D. Pandey and B. K. Tripathy, *op. cit.*, pp. 258-299; M. L. Bose, *British Relations with Tribes of North-East Frontier*, New Delhi, 1979, pp. 48-85 And Chandrika Singh, *Emergence of Arunachal Pradesh As A State*, Delhi, 1989, pp. 32-58.

Chapter - 5

Conclusion

History of a particular people is not overnight made. It is made brick by brick. It is the origin and clan structure of the people, their socio- politico- religious- cultural ethos which largely determine the course of history to be written on them. Documentation of all such ethos is an important tool of history. More is the documentation; merrier is the richness of history. People's contact and exposure with outside world happens to be the dynamic nomenclature to see history growing and gaining momentum. Human history is replete with all such examples. Civilizational habitations, structures, tools used, goods exchanged or traded, engineering and architectural skills, acumenship, entrepreneurship and their subsequent applications leave sufficient cornerstones at respective fields for history to shape leaving bias and prejudices apart. In a strictly logical view, the history of any country is an indivisible unity in which ideas, events, and personalities act and react on one another, often in an obscure and intangible manner. But such complex wholes do not lend themselves to clear exposition or convenient study until they are broken up into manageable units, and this process is bound to be somewhat arbitrary and conventional.

To reach at a particular hypothesis in the vast area of research we have to follow a critical and scientific evaluation of all sources at our disposal in the best possible manner. Instead of investigating the facts, already found and discussed, attention should be diverted for discovering some new sources with a view to finding out new ideas, concepts and data. Reconstruction rather than reproduction should be the prime object of research.

Writing of history in India has not been able to escape from the touch of prejudices. In the pre-independence era few historians branded as pro-British highlighted the contribution of Indian aristocrats and administrators who were Indian by birth but British by temperament. Instead of presenting the oppressive, exploitative and subjugating character of the British, directed the stream of history to be led on communal and unscientific lines.[1] But the independence of India brought about significant change in the approach of historiography. Devoid of biases and prejudices scientific approach to history in the areas of socio-economic movement of the general people, role of middle class, peasants, workers, slaves and a trend of writing regional history to supplement and compliment the national history started to set in.

Again, the role of the historian to thread the incidents of history into a form of history is equally significant. History becomes a study of reality in its aspect of becoming. The function of the historian is neither to love the past, nor to condemn the past, nor to be free from the past but to master the past in order to understand its bearing on the present. Historical activity involves three different types of functions which should be performed simultaneously. The first is to set at the truth, to know the entire human past as it actually happened and to be sure that solid facts are at hand. The second job is to interpret the facts, assess and evaluate and explain their significance. The third is to present the ideas in a clear and attractive manner. These three functions make the historian a scientist to gather facts, a philosopher to interpret them and a litterateur to express them. Hence given the discussion held above, the history of the origin of the different tribes needs to be highlighted for a kind of history to be placed before the readers written by a historian that we see and construe as the history of Arunachal Pradesh. Since the areas they occupied were covered with dense forests and rugged terrains, there could not be held any communication between the people of the plains and the tribes living in these areas.

Arunachal Pradesh has inspired because of its rare features administrators, historians, sociologists, anthropologists, political scientists and academia to observe, analyse, evaluate and present something about it. Because of lack of training in investigation methodology for objective research, certain constraints of financial and other resources, inaccessibility of the major areas of Arunachal etc., only a general overview not analytical but descriptive came out. Need was felt to deal with the socio-cultural, economic and political scenario of the state in new perspective, i.e. study of social institutions such as, nobles, middle-class, slaves and position of women; exposure and response syndrome of the people of Arunachal and socio-economic and political movements of its people.

The pre-independent period of Arunachal Pradesh witnessed the dark and gloomy days because the land and its people almost remained cut off from the outside world and were left in absolute isolation by several factors. Scope was limited for researchers of the other areas to come to the state to analyse its resources and present them in the form of history. The writers and historians during the British rule showed a keen interest in writing an elaborate and detailed history only of those regions which had vital importance from the administrative point of view which proved more congenial to accommodating expanding imperialist exploitative machinery. No doubt, the British Government was first to take a little bit of interest in collecting sources. However, such collection of sources suffered from some anomalies at its initial stage because the British collected primary sources from administrative point of view and not with the object of a proper and objective perspective. The British historiography on the whole could not overcome biases and prejudices inherent in the conceptual frameworks of the imperialist analysis. Naturally, the British collection and writings became susceptible to historical distortions.[2] Further, the British also had imposed restrictions for the outsiders to come to

Arunachal Pradesh during the early part of twentieth century. So, the concepts of the knowledge of civilization, social change and reformation etc. remained like anathema to the people of the state.

Being isolated for long and free from any interference from the people of the plains, these people established their respective tiny sovereign village states. Each of the tribes earmarked its territory by raising the boundary lines. Later on, they started their terrace and Jhum cultivation. "They established", as Chandrika Singh puts, "their rule on the basis of ancient Greek City State in the sense that a village state contained an organised political community". The customary laws and traditions took the place of their code of conducts. As they remained far from the modern civilisation and confined themselves to isolation, they never managed to "establish a single sovereign state of all the tiny village states". It is also a fact that due to their migration to the North East India in separate groups and their confinement to the different ridges covered with dense jungles, each group kept itself aloof from other with the result that variation took place in their respective culture, behaviours, customs, dialects and beliefs.

The reason why these tribal people migrated to this inhospitable and mountainous part of land appears to be the search for their livelihood. As Chandrika Singh puts, "They could have settled in the plains, but the plains area had already been occupied". The only vacant space for them was the hill areas. Therefore, they occupied the area and settled comfortably without any disturbances. Though the arrival of the Ahoms in the plains of Assam and their firmly established rule disturbed the isolation of those tribes who were living on the lower portion of these hills, it could not bring much difference in their internal life. It was the contact of the British with these people which in fact, brought about major changes in the traditional outlook and in political and economic life of the tribal people of the North east India."

The process of administrative and constitutional development of these tribes started about a century back when the British extended their administration to certain parts of this territory. But it gained momentum only after India's independence. The story of the political as well as administrative development of this area after independence is also a story of a search for and forging of a common personality by an assortment of people belonging to a number of tribes brought together by accident of history. At the time of independence other states and territories of India had their own identity developed through many decades or even centuries. Arunachal Pradesh however, then consisted of three artificially created administrative units, namely, the Balipara Frontier Tract, the Sadiya Frontier Tract, and the Tirap Frontier Tract, loosely administered by the British before independence as "Excluded Areas" under the Government of India Act, 1935. Each one of them was inhabited by a number of tribes or tribal groups having nothing in common except geographical proximity and ethnic similarity. Some of them were even antagonistic to each other. After independence the administration of these "Excluded Areas" passed on to the hands of Government of Assam but no change was brought in the quality of administration, except for bifurcation of the Sadiya Frontier Tract into two districts of the Abor Hills and the Mishmi Hills in 1948.

Situation of Arunachal Pradesh at that time presented a picture of a hilly terrain devoid of developed means of communication with a sparse population cut up into numerous isolated tribes or village communities. The people were mostly suspicious of outsiders like any other tribal people. The British had considered the area too backward and unrewarding for extending any civil administration there. Economically the area also did not prove to be profit- seeking. Rugged mountains, inaccessible forest-habitations, mighty rivers and rivulets with powerful gushing flow of water and unpredictable climatic schedule had left a withdrawal symptom with the British officials working in the region. The socio- political life of the tribes of the area therefore were untouched by any modernizing influence and remained primitive till the early years of independence of India.

Migration of these tribes to the present state of Arunachal and their subsequent settlement at different places led to the growth of different socio-economic, political and cultural ethos to determine the process of socialisation among them. Otherwise, given the diversity and insularity of the tribes the present day Arunachal bears, the state could have got dissipated much earlier, unlike the migration of the Aryans in the northern and the Dravidians in the southern India respectively. But the irony is that Arunachal goes to breast as much bulky a history as the north or south India has. Geography has played a great role in projecting enormously misbalanced weight of history across the country. It has rendered history uneven characteristics of growth and progress. Arunachal is certainly a victim of that. Much of its history has grown upon its people's social organization, political institutions, religious and cultural traditions. It is pertinent to know about them for associating them with the kind of history that should have grown up as we suppose to have been given the parameters of history to include them in its different phases.

If man is a social animal, the term 'social' can be defined to represent those qualities that render a man useful in the society and make him fit for human intercourse. Aristotle puts, "Man is fated to leave in a society and he needs other men in order to fulfil his spiritual essence". This opinion holds good even today, particularly in case of Arunachal where till very recently the modern materialistic values have not entered the society. The interdependence on one another was much more felt in this area than in most other parts of the country. Again, the culture of any people is a synthesis of the aspects of their social, educational, religious, artistic, economic and other activities and is a product of the struggle of mankind against the natural as well as manmade forces of the modern day. Convenience for methodology has led to the classification of culture as primitive, medieval or modern culture and the tribal culture of Arunachal has often been termed as primitive; the society as backward. This seems to be absolutely incorrect if we take the opinion of T. C. Hudson into account where he goes to say "The lower culture, in fact, is the basis of human societies".

One more opinion goes to say that the tribal society has changed little if at all over hundreds of years. This stands again incorrect. There remains no doubt that there had been a steady evolution of the tribal society and culture over the years. Further, the tribes of this region have another inheritance from the Mother Nature itself- the land and its climate. No study on the history of Arunachal can be said complete without keeping in mind the tough landscape and the extreme climate of this area that has shaped the society of the people. Due to absence of outside assistance the people learnt to cooperate by organizing themselves into a very cohesive village communities, which were in most of the cases, under a committee of locally respected elders, to care for almost every needs of the people. Thus, while trying to study the history and historiography of Arunachal, basing their society and culture as tools, we should not skip in our mind the tribal enduring, inheritance of climate, land and the fact that this region remained mostly cut away from the mainstream of the Indian society till very recently.

Standing isolated from the rest of the world for centuries and faced with extremely difficult living conditions, the tribals of this area have created a realistic picture of life as they face it with all its hardships, in their religion. Dr Verrier Elwin, in his book *A Philosophy for NEFA,* has pointed out five outstanding qualities of the religious system of NEFA. Firstly there is a very general belief in a Supreme God who is just, benevolent and good; secondly, in the tribal religion there is a genuine emphasis in the spiritual realities behind the events of everyday life; thirdly, the tribal religion is built from an elaborate mythology; fourthly, the tribal religion is associated with a social ethic that unites the tribe in its discipline, and finally, the tribal religion gives the people the power to reconcile themselves in the eternal emergencies of life. We can add one more quality to it, i.e., unlike many other religions of the world, the tribal religion is not a separate institution in itself controlled by a particular section of the society. Their religion is a part of their everyday life, not confined to the shrines or temples only. It has simple ethical codes that unite the people and inspire the tribal qualities of hospitality, simplicity, truthfulness and integrity.

The history of Arunachal Pradesh was largely influenced by the twin interests of the British, i.e., colonial interest in the Brahmaputra Valley and imperial commercial interest beyond the frontiers. The process of economic and political incorporation of the Arunachal hills had started with the extension of the British rule in the valley. While the former was manifested mainly through a change in the nature and extent of frontier trade, the latter through the establishment of the British political supremacy and colonial legitimacy. Apart from interest on tea, the discovery of coal and petroleum in 1825 in the valley and subsequent development of mining and extraction activities- all these had attracted a huge investment of capital which had been the monopoly of the European merchants and demanded security from the turbulent tribal communities surrounding the valley. But the tea-planters' influence in the valley was so strong that the civil and military elements stood subservient to the interests of them.

Hence, by the early twentieth century, the British had succeeded largely to establish their political supremacy and colonial legitimacy among the hill tribes of the frontier. A few tribes were even brought under direct rule. Permanent administrative centres had been established at Pasighat and Nizamghat (shattered during the 1950 earthquake). During 1917-18 all the Khamptis were assessed to poll tax and treated as full- fledged British subjects. In 1941 a permanent Assam Rifles outpost was established at Rupa and during 1945-46 Sherdukpens, Monpas and some Khowas (Buguns) were brought under tax network (House Tax). In fact, with the delineation of Inner Line in 1873 and Mc Mahon Line in 1914, the tract lying between these two lines roughly corroborates the area of the present day Arunachal Pradesh, the process of political incorporation of the Arunachal hills into the British Indian empire took a definite shape which facilitated the quick political integration of the frontier with independent India.

When we start to study the history of Arunachal Pradesh we find scant written record available. Absence of a script among the tribes inhabiting the region has been a major drawback for documenting aspects of tribal life for their presentation before the readers in black and white. The history of the region, hence, becomes all the more patchy and fragmented. But the written record has not been the only source of seeking information about the progress and development of the mankind- the subject matter of history. No doubt, there are certain handicaps in reconstructing the history of Arunachal Pradesh; yet there are a number of sources that help us to a considerable extent to draw an account of the area.

A survey of all such prehistoric findings in Arunachal reveals that most of the finds are exploratory in nature, without any stratigraphic context. Only Parsi- Parlo site gives us an idea of culture development from a Ceramic Neolithic to Ferrolithic stage. However, various palaeolithic tools from Daphabhum and single specimen from Pagam in Lower Subansiri area along with evidence of fossil in Arunachal indicate the existence of Lower Palaeolithic Culture here. In 1974-75 first ever vertebrate fossils, viz., the molar of *Bos* has been unearthed by the Geological Survey of India from the upper tertiary horizon of Eastern Himalayas, in the Ramghat area of the Lower Subansiri within Arunachal Pradesh. This discovery is of considerable importance, establishing the continuation of the Western Siwaliks, where similar findings are noticeable, bearing similar palaeo-environs. Thus the upper tertiary horizon of Arunachal can be recognized like the Western Siwaliks, as the probable habitation of the area of the Hominids and Paleolithic man.

Most of the stone tools recovered from the state show Neolithic features. Though various Neolithic implements are noticed, pottery of the period is very few. Only one site Parsi-Parlo has yielded a few potsherds from stratified deposits, revealing its affinity with Chinese and South East Asian pottery. Comparative study of materials and technology exhibits close affinity of the neoliths of Arunachal with the objects of Assam, Burma, Indo-China, China and Malay Peninsula. No proof of iron or copper age culture in Arunachal has so far been made. The combined evidence of ethnology and archaeology, i.e., a clear correlation between a particular type of Neolithic Celt viz., the shouldered and polished variety with Austro-Asialitic languages amply suggests that the Austronesians were responsible for the development of Neolithic cultures in the North East India, the very first region through which it entered. Even the beliefs and practices of the present day tribal people of Arunachal have a similarity with that of the Burmese and other people of South East Asian countries in relation to these prehistoric tools. The tribes of Arunachal cherish Neoliths as charms and occasionally use them as amulets to ward off different kind of calamities and evils.

From the above discussion, it appears that Palaeolithic people had their habitation in this region. Like that the Neolithic culture in this religion does not seem to have an independent origin and typologically this culture comes closer to that of South East Asia. Ecological, linguistic and other historical evidences seem to indicate that this part was penetrated by prehistoric people from Yunan and Burma. It is noteworthy to mention here that the state still bears the cultural and economic pattern of the Neolithic people.

All such widely scattered archaeological remains at different places in Arunachal bear testimony to its rich cultural heritage. Excavations at Bhismaknagar in Dibang Valley which was once a strong-hold of the Chutiyas of Assam between twelfth to sixteenth centuries A.D. reveal the high standard of civilization that once prevailed in the state in ancient times. Forts of Bhalukpong in the West Kameng district and of Itanagar so far yielding a few stone terracotta and metal figures, demonstrate various phases of cultural movements in Arunachal. Migration of different ethnic groups, their admixture and cultural contact with the world beyond its present geographical limits are vividly recorded amid the sculptural treasures as well as in other material remains which show rich sense of historicity.

Inscriptions found within the boundaries of present day Arunachal so far known do not go beyond the fourteenth century A.D. Their short cryptic nature does not cite good details required for building up a satisfactory account of the territory based alone on their evidence. Still, the hidden truth of the epigraphic documents certainly renders them valuable as bedrocks of history of their respective periods offering definite information. Some of these bear specific dates while in case of others palaeography and circumstantial evidence help to ascertain their time and place of origin with a tolerant amount of certainty. Although the known specimens are very few in number, they offer some variety in language and script as well as in their subject matter. These are variously written in Assamese- Bengali, Tibetan, Newari, Tai and Burmese scripts. Even Sanskrit has been used on Assamese-Bengali characters. They need to be focused and harnessed properly for their relevance in the history of Arunachal Pradesh.

There is almost a complete absence of literary sources of history in the regional languages of Arunachal Pradesh. Since most of the tribes lack a script, they have not been able to preserve any recorded history, exceptions being the Khamptis of the Lohit district and the Monpas of the Kameng district. The Khamptis, who came to Assam in the later part of the eighteenth century possess a script derived originally from the Tai language. The Khampti literature mainly deals with Buddhist tenets, way of life, cosmology and mythology. There is one Khampti manuscript which contains a complete criminal code, enumerating punishments for both trivial and serious offences. The Khamptis also maintained some form of historical records called *Chyatuie*, which consists of writings on law, social and political events. But unfortunately, these sources more or less remain to be explored.

The Monpas of Kameng have been able to preserve many canonical literature of the Mahayana School of Buddhism like *Tanjur* and *Kanjur* in the Tibetan script in various ancient monasteries including the Great Tawang Monastery. The monasteries are also said to have preserved some records in the form of account books, agreements, sanads and parwanas. However, all these Khampti and Monpa regional literature provides useful references about the people, their contacts with Burma and China respectively and their religious activities.

The pre-independent India witnessed publication of some of the important monographs on this region. W. Robinson's "*A Descriptive Account of Assam*", London, 1841, A. Hamilton's "*In Abor Jungle*", London, 1912, R.S. Kennedy's "*Ethnological Report on the Akas, Khowas, Mijis and Membas of Tawang*", Shillong, 1914 and Robert Reid's "*History of the Frontier Areas bordering Assam from 1883-1941*", Shillong, 1942 stood as milestones for the study of the region. But the Indian independence brought a new era to this isolated land taking research on the area to a level. Scholars particularly administrators, anthropologists and sociologists carried on research publications on the historiography of Arunachal in 1950's and 60's. Some of the works published during this period may be discussed for the well corroboration of the facts. "*The Hidden Land*", London, 1953 by Graham Bower, "*Myths of the North-East Frontier of India*", Shillong, 1958, "*Democracy in NEFA*", Shillong, 1958, "*A Philosophy for NEFA*", Shillong, 1959, "*India's North-East Frontier in the 19th Century*", Bombay, 1959, "*Arts and Crafts of the North-Eastern Frontier of India*", Shillong, 1959 and "*India's North-East Frontier in the 19th Century*", Bombay, 1959 by Verrier Elwin; "*Anthropology and Administration in the Tribal Areas of the North-East Frontier*", 1949, "*Himalayan Barbary*", London, 1955 and "*The Apa Tanis and their Neighbours*", London, 1962 by C. von Furer-Haimendorf; "*The Daflas of the Subansiri Region*", Shillong, 1959 and "*The Sherdukpens*", Shillong, 1961 by R.R.P. Sharma; "*A Ceremonial Ox of India- The Mithun in Nature, Culture and History*", Madison, 1963 by F.J. Simoons; and "*Demographic and Socio-Economic Profiles of the Hill Areas of North-East India*", New Delhi, 1961 by B.K. Roy Burman are some of the works. Further, three outstanding historians, S.K. Bhuyan, K.N. Dutt and H.K. Barpujari started writing on modern history after 1951when contributions in modern history were made for the first time in the Jaipur session of the Indian History Congress by the scholars of this region (K.N. Dutt and H.K. Barpujari).[3]

The Chinese aggression dawned significant changes in the historiography of Arunachal. It baffled not only the planners and administrators but also the historians and other social scientists. Arunachal became the cynosure of their inspiration and investigation, the cockpit of historical sources and hypotheses. A good deal of works which came out in 1970's and 80's highlighting the social, cultural, political and economic history of Arunachal are- "*British Policy in NEFA*", New Delhi, 1979 by M.L. Bose; "*Tribal History and Civilization of the People of Assam to the Twelfth Century A.D.*", Guwahati, 1966, "*A Comparative Study of Adi Religion*", Shillong, 1971, "*Arunachal Panorama*", Shillong, 1973, "*Arunachal Through the Ages*", New Delhi, 1982 and "*Arunachal from Frontier Tract to Union Territory*", New Delhi, 1983 by J.N. Chowdhury; "*Arunachal Tattoo*", Census of India, 1971, New Delhi, 1975 by I.K. Barthakur; "*Modernization and Elites in Arunachal Pradesh*", Census of India, 1971, New Delhi, 1975 by S.M. Dubey; *"The Problem of Change: A Study of North-East India",* Delhi, 1987 by B.P. Singh; "*Highlanders of Arunachal Pradesh*", New Delhi, 1982 by C. von Furer-Haimendorf; "*Wealth of Arunachal Pradesh*", Guwahati, 1978, "*Arunachal Pradesh: Rich Land and Poor People*", Guwahati, 1986 and "*Socio-Economic and Demographic Dimensions of Arunachal Pradesh*", Guwahati, 1988 by S.D. Jha and "*Social and Economic Profile of North-East India*", Delhi, 1978 by B. Dutta Ray (ed).

The political history and social administration of different social institutions of Arunachal have been carried to the vast platform of research, but only the outlines have emerged so far. Elaborate studies of the centripetal manifestation of the social administrative machinery along with its consequences and tensions and their repercussion on the policies and propaganda of various political and social institutions are yet to be traced out in proper perspective. Social hierarchy has created ample scope to be highlighted in the big platform of research. Scholars have hardly carried about subaltern studies on different tribes and sub-tribes of the state.

Contemporary history is no less important than past history. In most of the independent countries it is not a taboo. But the British Government and historians had always discouraged it and the contemporary records were not made accessible by them to the Indian researchers for fear that the contemporary history may give rise to controversies and criticism of the colonial regime and strengthen the turbulent forces of nationalism and finally make the British position unstable and dilapidating. Consequently, the historians of India never wrote history of contemporary happenings and movements. Hence, there is a rich field for research on contemporary history.[4]

Long contact with Bhutan, Tibet and Burma and 'Exposure and Response' to the developing and developed situations of these areas to the people of the rest part of India have prioritised the studies in research. The attempt to chalking out the dimensions of the 'Exposure and Response' is not at all a herculean task but they can be proved a prospective sequel to begin with. Since there existed a direct and harmonious exposure of Arunachal with the neighbouring parts of India, i.e., Tibet, Bhutan and Myanmar because of its same ethnicity, it was quite natural for a regular cultural assimilation to grow. But the mode of cultural interaction was too slow in countryside of Arunachal because of its impenetrable, harsh diverse parts. So, definite studies are expected to propel us to understand the complex social structure of the tribes the state.

People's oral recall of their past has been the most productive source of information, especially for the relatively recent past. The human memories may relate to relatively to recent events, experienced by persons now alive, or these may recall events whose memory has been transmitted through the generations down to one's informants. A corpus of material transmitted orally for generations, may reach the historian in this form.[5] It may be noted here that the methodology of the use of taped interviews to document the Oral history for research which was once considered to be the safest and comfortable mode in the last several decades has undergone sea-change with the insurrection of the modern technology in the recent days. This fascinating method of advanced technology now forms a popular means to harvest in detail the special flavour of an earlier, nearly forgotten past.

Problems and limitations do go hand in glove while conducting interviews. One could use a tech-savvy recorder only after a certain rapport had been established between the interviewer and the informants. And if one does not know the language of the area under study, one has to rely on the interpreters who often fail to give all details passed by the informants while being interviewed. Sometimes an interpreter only summarises by the village-respondent while interpreting. He may skip information on what he considers irrelevant or redundant. If an interpreter is found to be prejudiced, he may even suppress the information diluting the essential features of the study. The same is also true in case of the informants who may sometimes deliberately give wrong information and suppress the truth. It is not possible therefore to rely solely on oral testimony for historical research. But where the local records are available, cross checks and supplements to local interviews can be made scientifically.

For carrying out research on various changes of the societies of Arunachal the folklores and oral traditions of the respective tribes may play a great role because if history is the mother of truth, folklore happens to be the mother of emancipation and reconstruction. Though initiatives have been taken by Sachin Roy, Professor T. Mibang and Dr. T. Nyori and others, much more is to be done in this regard because to set right the distortions, the history of Arunachal analysed through folklores and oral traditions is expected to be of much use.

With the advent of the British a new trend was set in history writing. Most of the English writers were not professional historians; but basically administrators or military officers. Their knowledge of the North East and its people proved milestone for compilation of a number of worthy historical works. The beginning was made by J. P. Wade accompanying Captain Welsh to Assam in 1792 as a doctor who compiled his translated version of Assamese Buranjis titled *An Account of Assam* together with a graphic geographical account captioned *A Geographical Sketch of Assam.*

Another very redeeming feature of nineteenth century historiography is the publication of scores of books and accounts on the frontier tribes. The students of tribal history today recall with gratitude the contributions made by some European officers towards advancement of historical studies. Their intimate knowledge of the tribal customs and institutions and their exploratory habits always placed them on a more advantageous position than the native writers. The result was the production of some highly informative narratives on almost all the major tribes of North East India. Arunachal stood no exception to it.

Even some of the works based on expeditional experiences prove to be worthy primary sources to decipher important information about the tribes during the period. Researchers are immensely benefited by such works to reach out closest to the facts available in the then period for placing them on records further with different research orientation and interpretation required in today's world. That is how Arunachal is still considered as the treasure-house of knowledge. Its unique social, religious, cultural, lingual and ethnic dialectics with tribal heterogeneity have attracted many a scholars to delve deep into such ever-exploring social phenomena.

Large number of documents written and compiled by the British Officers in the colonial period, both civil and military, on their interaction with the various tribes of Arunachal stand milestone as historiographical compendium projecting the geographical, climatic and the laws and customs of the people. The publication of monographs on various hill tribes of North east India is one of the most outstanding contributions of the British towards the understanding of the tribes of the hills. With the gradual extension of their power over these hills, the British came into more contact with these diverse hill people and felt it necessary to know more about them for effective administration.

Arunachal Pradesh (earlier NEFA), though treated as a land of insularity, had invited the attention of the British since the beginning of the British rule in India. Reports on the tribes of the state were prepared even before the annexation of Assam to the Company's territories. Great task was endorsed by the Company to Francis Hamilton (later known as Buchanon Hamilton) and R. B. Pemberton to prepare reports on the provinces on the Frontiers of Bengal. After Assam being annexed, the British officers, civil and military, posted in Assam were asked to prepare reports on the frontier tribes and the officers recorded their exploratory reports which though biased and fell short of introspection, stand cynosure for providing valuable information on the different aspects of tribal life in the state of the time.

Though the colonial rule never attempted to prepare a synchronized account of the different tribes of the Frontier region, efforts were made from 1881 onwards to include monographs on the Frontier tribes in the Census of India Reports. Thus, by 1947 all but the tribes of the western hills and those who lived on the fringes of the border were covered in these reports. But such reports were found suffering from inaccuracy, particularly in respect of statistical data, as none of the officers went inside the hills to collect them. But monographs and different accounts on different tribes although biased began to appear. "Such bewildering mass of reports and accounts of various kinds are elusive, some are biased, others suffer from lack of understanding, and a few are partial and incomplete", writes M. L. Bose. Despite criticisms being labeled against such works published and documented during colonial period by the British officials on Arunachal Pradesh, they are considered as the basic and solid sources of historiography for carrying out interdisciplinary research on the heterogeneous tribal societies in all their aspects of the contemporary period and beyond, with exceptions of skeptic misunderstanding on the varied nature of the tribes, sub-tribes, clan structure and names of the places.

Apart from the above literature various unpublished works like Political Proceedings, Secret Proceedings, Official Correspondences and Revenue Proceedings, Census Reports, Military Reports of the British period serve as primary source for the study of the history of Arunachal. These various unpublished documents can be studied in the National Archives, New Delhi; the Asiatic Society of Bengal, Kolkata; the National Library, Kolkata; and the Assam Secretariat Record Office, Guwahati etc. All these documents along with the various published monographs mentioned above give us almost an overall scenario of the social, political, economic and cultural history Arunachal.

To conduct historical research in Arunachal Pradesh has been found to be very difficult since materials, written or unwritten, relating to the history of this area other than some oral literature and a number of historical ruins lying in the foot hills of the territory are practically not available. Initially up to 1865, the scholars knew of only three ruins namely, Bhalukpong in the West Kameng District and Tamreswari temple and Bhismaknagar in the Lohit District. But as a result of subsequent explorations and excavations a good number of other such ruins dating approximately from the early Christian era have been brought to light. Hence, it will not be exaggeration to say that the history of Arunachal Pradesh is mixed with legends, folklores and traditional accounts. Much of the history of Arunachal Pradesh has so far remained hidden. There is a dearth of historical materials of the socio-political history of the source materials pertaining to the socio-political conditions of the state.

Arunachal Pradesh, the so-called North East Frontier Agency (NEFA) in the colonial period, was a closed land in the sense that travelling across the Inner Line was not allowed. Even now a person other than the Arunachalis desiring to visit the state in any capacity has to obtain an Inner Line Pass, issued temporarily from the competent authority. Such passes were also issued during the British regime; but generally, except for Europeans the land remained virtually hidden behind an iron curtain, and all sorts of mysterious and absurd stories were associated with the life and culture of the tribes living in it. In the nineteenth century, as also in the early twentieth, a thorough study of the culture of the Indian people was undertaken by nationalist scholars and the past was glorified. But the frontiers still remained in isolation. The state remained out of the stream of India's national development.

The attempt of the British historians, administrators, anthropologists, geographers and scholars during the colonial period to write on the tribes, geography and environment of present day Arunachal, despite constraints of availability of source materials and topographical hazards is noteworthy, if tested through a balance parameter of research. Biases are many. Prejudices follow the same. Colonial interests too go side by side. But carrying an orientation towards writing, publishing and documenting something to be bequeathed for posterity on the state during the colonial period ask the scholars to retrospect on the issue.

Politically and culturally the state was still in her ancient character up to the early years of India's independence. It is difficult to trace out the relations of the Arunachal tribes with the outside world prior to the sixteenth century A.D. due to want of any authentic record. One of the key factors which regulated these relations was the tough topography of Arunachal and the lack of some of the daily necessities of life in this area, such as salt, iron and clothes etc. To meet these requirements they had to depend on the plains. Hence they frequently raided the plains and obtained these articles by force. It was the reason why the Ahom ruler Pratap Singha (1603-1641) introduced one 'Posa' system as means of compensation to the tribes to protect the subjects of the plains from the raids.

The British developed their relations with Arunachal Pradesh in different phases. In the Western side, while they started developing relations with the Akas as early as 1825, with the Sherdukpens as early as 1836 and the Bhutias as early as 1838, in the Central region, their relations began with the Adis as early as 1825, with the Nyishis as early as 1835 and with the Apatanis as early as 1895 and in the Eastern side, they had their relations with Mishmis and Singphos as early as 1825 and with the Khamptis as early as 1830.

At the time of independence Arunachal Pradesh consisted of three artificially created administrative units, namely, the

Balipara Frontier Tract, the Sadiya Frontier Tract, and the Tirap Frontier Tract. They were loosely administered by the British before Independence as *'Excluded Areas'* under the Government of India Act, 1935. Each one of them was inhabited by a number of tribes or tribal groups having nothing in common except geographical proximity and ethnic similarity. The British had considered the area too backward and unrewarding for extending any civil administration, except that for bifurcating the Sadiya Frontier into two districts of the Abor Hills and the Mishmi Hills in 1948. Despite the state being assessed unrewarding for the British, rewarding was their earnest attempt to generate some amount of literature in the then period which rolls into the fold of historiography now. Let us now bring about a review of the same which largely covers the area of the paper under discussion.

Periodisation of the history of Arunachal Pradesh on the basis of the historical sources available, considered so far being very scanty and inadequate, in the line of the conventional pattern of Ancient, Medieval and Modern as the history of a particular state of our country goes, is not so easy a profession. Acute dearth of sources renders scholars handicap in pushing the phases of history of Arunachal into the parameter of justification of phases of Indian History. Still, for the sake of convenience of the readers reconstruction of history of Arunachal into Ancient, Medieval and Modern has been suitably made by the scholars, not in congruence with the parameter of division of Indian history.

It is believed as per the ruins of buildings excavated and legends prevalent that ancient Arunachal Pradesh had almost eight kingdoms namely Prabhu Mountain, Prabhu Kuthara, Bidarbha, Chedi, Bhalukpong, Malinithan, Kalita and Gomsi (Rani) on which little discussion is held above. But no definite length of period has yet been ascertained as to when all these ancient kingdoms flourished and when decayed. As discussed in the beginning dearth of historical records has rendered the ancient history of the state obscure. The Puranic literature, legends, myths and local says have pushed such history to an extent which it is presently found to be. Logical exposition of truth is traced out on the basis of the little historical and archaeological materials deciphered so far. But it does not fit into the logical and inquisitive minds of scholars of history. The issue of the royal dialectics under the purview of a historical diaspora in the form of king- kingdom relationship has been found to be a great missing link to make the history as found more sound and logistic as compared to history of the time in respect of other states in India. There is not an ounce of negativism displayed so far from any quarter to render such history more dynamism. But topographical bottlenecks, communicational handicaps and situational restrictions have worked hand in hand from time to time to place such history in a shape we are to be satisfied with, before the readers and scholars.

It is therefore, believed that the ancient Arunachal Pradesh was probably either an ally of Kamrupa or it acknowledged the suzerainty of the ancient Kamrupa. Mystery so far has not been unearthed to determine the history of the ancient Arunachal. Limited sources throw very grey ray on its history. The Ahom-tribal relationship goes to suggest that the different tribes of Arunachal had their relations with the Ahom administration ranging from the fag end of fifteenth century to the beginning of nineteenth century, i.e; from 1487 whereby Tangsas could be found raiding the plains of Assam during the reign of the Ahom ruler Susenpha (1439-1488) to 1807 whereby the Noctes raiding the plains of Assam during the reign of the Ahom ruler Kamaleshwar Singha (1795-1811).

The modern history of Arunachal Pradesh begins with the annexation of Assam by the British in 1826 after the Treaty of Yandaboo which opened up a new chapter in the history of North East India as whole. The previous regime of the Ahoms lasted over the Brahmaputra valley for over six centuries (1228-1826). By the end of eighteenth century the kingdom was in the crater of an internal rebellion which weakened it substantially. The Burmese desire for eastward expansion fuelled by royal intrigue in the Ahom Court led to the Burmese invasion in 1819. Ravaged by the Burmese insurrection the weakened Ahom monarch turned to the East India Company seeking its aid to deal with the situation. The Anglo– Burmese War which was ensued got concluded with the signing of the Treaty of Yandaboo. The legacy of the undefined and bedeviled relations of the Ahom kings with the tribes of Arunachal was over. The British stepped into the shoes of Ahoms and inherited from the latter a legacy of relationship with the hill tribes of present Arunchal Pradesh.

The above discussion capsuled under modern period of history of Arunachal suggests that the British tribal relationship started as early as 1825 once the British had footage in Assam after the First Anglo- Burmese War. One thing which seems to be very transparent is that it was the Ahom legacy bequeathed to the British to maintain their nexus with the tribes of the North East in as insular way as had been maintained so far with Arunachal posing no extraordinary exception before them. A patchwork policy could only be initiated, executed and maintained. The incessant tribal threats in terms of frequent raids on the plains of Assam resorting sometimes to the British objectionable phenomena like loot, kidnap and murder often put them in an administrative mesh. Given the geographical and topographical hazards and nature's often unpredictable challenges that the then Arunachal threw before them, for a trading company like that of the British East India Company which had profit as one of its cynosure- policies to spend pies on journey, survey, expedition and above all on maintaining relations with tribes living beyond their comfort-eye-contact perception to the exclusion of the phenomena mentioned above, has to be construed critically. Of course, things started changing with the onset of the twentieth century. British orientation towards Arunachal got a preponderant importance once the Chinese frowning eyes on the north of present Arunachal started distracting their comfort-eye-contact perception. The murder of Noel Williamson in 1911 seconded it and alarmed them to streamline a clear-cut border policy towards Arunachal.

Periodisation is an attempt to categorize or divide historical time into discrete named blocks. It is a complex problem in history and is expected to remain so from a historian's own level of exposition. Of course, it is a historian's liberty how he looks at a fact and how he relates it to a specific block of history. Generally, the historian with the help of available primary and secondary sources reconstructs the history of any country. As history is not a simple narration of events in a chronological and spatial order, the historian has to choose the sources that are authentic and can be corroborated by other sources before arriving at a historical generalisation. As the contemporary approach to history is to understand the historical process and attempt to explain it in the present times, a historian should be knowledgeable about theories of historical method as well as of other social sciences. It is essential to develop the needed analytical skills of source materials objectively before the historical process is constructed.

History is in fact continuous, and so all systems of periodisation are to some extent arbitrary. Almost every dynamic age is an "age of transition" as the cliché has it. It is nevertheless necessary to divide up history in order to make sense of the past and to articulate changes over time. Furthermore, different nations and cultures experience different histories of their own, and so do they require different models of periodisation. Periodising labels are challenged and being challenged and redefined all the time. Thus a historian may claim that there was no such thing as the Renaissance, while others may develop the logic to defend the concept. The reasons for this are believed to be complex. Periodising blocks will inevitably overlap, interlace or even seemingly contradict one another. Some have a cultural usage i.e. "the Gilded Age", others refer to prominent historical events like "the Inter-War years: 1918–1939", yet others are defined by decimal numbering systems like "the 1960s", "the seventeenth century" etc. Other periods are named from influential or talismanic individuals ("the Victorian Era", "the Edwardian Era", "the Napoleonic Era"). Again, certain periodising concepts only apply under specific conditions. Some of these usages are also to be geographically specific. This is especially true of periodizing labels derived from individuals or ruling dynasties, such as the

Jacksonian Era in America, the Meiji Era in Japan, or the Merovingian Period in France.

The model of periodization that is now-a-days hegemonic in Indian history squarely based on the colonial model first articulated by James Mill, is both heuristically unsatisfactory and politically unviable. From a heuristic viewpoint, it refers only to the 'religious' composition of the 'ruling class' (and, by the way, not even the whole of the ruling class). This tripartite division of Indian history on religious and ethnic nature of rulers as Hindu, Muslim and British does not seem to be precise as all the rulers in the Hindu period were not Hindus and we have a number of rulers who migrated to India from other countries and ruled side by side with the Hindu rulers and the Hindus were not culturally a homogenous entity either. Further, this division is not acceptable to modern historians as it has communal tinge which is not desirable for a pluralistic country like India. But there are still some historians who believe in that division.

From a political viewpoint, it stresses the divisive elements present in the Indian historical tradition, by implicitly equating 'Hindu' with 'Indian' and 'Muslim' with 'invader or foreigner'. A scientifically more inclusive and politically less dangerous new model needs to be sketched out by building on the assumption that Indian history is part of world history and, consequently, that the main socio-economic developments in the Indian subcontinent are part and parcel of the most relevant socio-economic developments world-wide. The model may de-emphasize the temporal divisive elements of the Indian experience, represented by the separate religious strands historically present within the Indian society. Focusing on socio-economic evolution may probably make both the fundamental unity of Indian history and its relationship with the history of the remainder of the world obvious. In the last few decades, there is a revisiting of periodisation by the histo-rians because new questions are asked and new sources are consulted and collated to arrive at conclusions regarding the factors of change that necessitated new socio-economic formations that led to new cultural and political patterns that shaped the course of our historical process.

However, for the sake of convenience, periodisation has been taken as necessary and the historians have broadly divided the entire range of Indian history into three periods i.e., Hindu, Muslim and British or the more appropriate divisions like Ancient, Medieval and Modern. But there is no consensus among the historians to fix the border line between these periods. There will indeed be some uncertainty over where the ancient period ends and the medieval begins, but the three phase periodisation is retained with a difference of a few centuries by one and all.

The threefold division of Indian history into ancient, medieval and modern periods owes much to post Renaissance European self perception of its own history. Periodisation is necessarily concerned with change. A society's history cannot be periodised if it did not undergo changes that too qualitative ones. Thus even while it was possible to divide Indian history on the basis of dynasties that ruled, it was difficult to talk in terms of modes of production and social formations. The ambitious task Kosambi had outlined for Indian historians – to present 'in chronological order of successive changes in the means and relations of production' still remains a query like task.

Hence history has not been primarily about isolated 'facts' or details. It tries to select, arrange, analyse and explain them through narratives which are diverse, change- seeking, often mutually conflicting. Relativistic doubts and questionings do not stand entirely irrelevant here. A bit of information about the past becomes a historical 'fact' only within a particular narrative, which would be based on a set of hypotheses or frame of analysis. In a sense, then, it is 'constituted' by the latter. Of course, it depends largely on the historian how he encashes his knowledge on the information towards presenting it into a flair-led historical asset.

This three phase division got entrenched in the school and university education so much so that it continues to this day. Part of the reason was that it neatly matched the three year school and undergraduate courses in history. So the threefold division was retained with a little shifting of the dates to give it a veneer of secularism. Thus instead of commencing the medieval period with the establishment of Muslim rule in 1190, the 'cut- off point' was shifted to the death of Harshavardhana around circa 650 CE. This interestingly was supposed to mark the end of large empires and the beginning of feudalism.

To see history and time valid and valuable, past is periodised or divided into different units of time variously called eras, epochs or periods. They serve as important conceptual tools to grasp and comprehend the vast temporal stretch of human history. However, periodising history is not a simple task. First, there are conceptual difficulties in abstraction and generalization. The problem hinges around the question of locating indicators or variables that determine change in history, which also help draw a dividing line between eras, and thus demarcate one historical period from another. Here it does not seem out of place to recall M. Morony's note of caution to historians, who maintains that the apparent cultural and institutional inertia that is generally taken to be continuity in history, is nothing but a slow and gradual change.

Secondly, the whole process of periodisation has been politicized. At times the criterion of periodising history might be consciously or unconsciously politically driven. So the construction of a historical period may reflect the hidden prejudices of its formulators. Since historical periods are generally taken for granted, their informal citing becomes a source of encouraging the biases and prejudices.

Thirdly, since the periodisation of history is firmly rooted in academic traditions, it restricts historical thinking and imagination. One also finds oneself confined in its conceptual barrier. As generally people tend to think within their given categories, it becomes difficult to transcend the conceptual categories of periodisation and go beyond them. Referring to this 'rigidifying power of periodisation', William Green has rightly put: "Once firmly drawn and widely accepted, period frontiers can become intellectual straitjackets that profoundly affect our habits of mind—the way we retain images, make associations, and perceive the beginning, middle and ending of things."

Lastly, as seen, some of the notions on historical periodisation have gone bulky. With the change of time, a thick layer of interpretation has got sedimented on them, making them heavy, biased and politically-backed. Their non-academic use has put the scholars in a fix for their scholarly interpretation as one of the sources of historiography. They have lost their neutrality as concepts. Presently, periodisation of history as units of historical studies has gained varied connotations, the most common being the tripartite scheme of ancient-medieval-modern periods in consonance with the dominant standard periodisation of European history since the eighteenth century going by the nomenclature, the Ancient, Medieval and Modern, followed by the colonial scheme of partition, putting 'Yes' to it, of the history of the colonized regions in Africa and Asia, including India.

At the turn of the twentieth century, the ancient-medieval-modern scheme of division of Indian history was adopted in South Asia, which replaced the Orientalists' triadic formulation of Hindu, Muslim, and British periods of Indian history. The term 'Medieval India' went by the name 'Muslim India', as interpreted by the Orientalists. In fact, the so-called Hindu, Muslim and British periods roughly correspond with the ancient, medieval and modern eras of Indian history. In contemporary South Asian historiographical traditions, the latter chronological constructs are now commonly used as convenient labels. The medieval period in Indian history, as in European history, is often referred to as the 'Middle Ages'. It is understood as a post-classical age denoting a radical shift from ancient or classical period. Moreover, there seems to be an inherent bias in it, as it implies decline and degeneration in medieval times as opposed to the splendour and glory of the ancient past.

The periodisation of Indian history into three periods, i.e., Hindu, Muslim and British can be traced back to the historian James Mill's *History of British India*. This kind of classification is based on the nationality or religions of the ruling class which rendered a communal rendition to the Indian history. This seems to have been, as if, forcibly rent jeopardising the inherent flow of structuralism in history. However, such periodisation was followed by the historians until some historians questioned its validity and significance. At present mostly the scholars use the nomenclature, Ancient, Medieval and Modern in place of Hindu, Muslim and British in periodising Indian history. But there is no unanimity among the historians regarding the exact terminal date of these periods. Generally, it is construed that Ancient period begins with the Harappan Culture from C.2500 B.C. and ends with C.1000 A.D. or 1200 A.D. The advent of Muslims as the most dominating political power in India is accepted as the end of the ancient period and the beginning of the medieval period. The year 1757 is generally taken as the end of the medieval period and the beginning of the modern. The Battle of Plassey was definitely a turning point in Indian history since it offered the British a strong footage to hegemonise their political power over Bengal, a strong state of the eighteenth century India.

Even if we accept in a broader framework these terminating dates for the division of the Ancient, Medieval and Modern periods of Indian history, it cannot be applied fully to the regional history, specifically to the history of Deccan and South India, Eastern, north-eastern and frontier India. Whatever way the periodisation in Indian history has been made, it is mainly based on the history of the Northern India with its geographical thrust on the Ganges valley. Looking at the structure of history of the whole of India such division is not acceptable, because there is no uniform and common date for the establishment of Muslim rule in India. The arrival of Muslims in different parts varies from time to time which raises question of validity of transition of regional history from Ancient to Medieval. Similarly, the foundation of British rule which is taken as the beginning of the Modern period varies at different regions of India asking the historians to believe in a different period of beginning of the Modern history.

It is clear that chronology is the only tool by which periodisation of even regional history can be validated. But unfortunately history of Arunachal Pradesh does not have a chronological sequence of historical process and development. History of Arunachal gives altogether a different picture which does not conform to aforesaid characteristics of periodisation. A good work of history starts with the collection of relevant historical material from different sources. This constitutes the first step of historical research, the second stage being the analytical operation of materials. The systematic arrangement of raw materials is the third step of the same, while the final construction by the synthetic operation and exposition is the last stage in historical research. Having considered briefly the process of conducting historical research, the historian has to seek, select, analyse, compare, construct, reconstruct and review the past from the varied sources.

So far as the early history of the people of Arunachal Pradesh in Ancient India is concerned, it is scanty and sparse having no chronology at all compared to other regional early history while its immediate border state Assam then named Kamarupa or Pragjyotisha possesses a strong early history in Ancient India with sources and chronology with which Arunachal had accessibility excepting certain stray references of mythological narratives and archaeological remains of present day Arunachal. Even no radio carbon dating has so far been made possible in the region to ascertain the age of the palaeolithic sites deciphered in some of the regions which is discussed in the later lines.

All these discussions go to suggest that there was no fixed chronological date which could be put into the framework of ancient Indian history of Arunachal Pradesh compared to the historical process taking place in northern India according to which periodisation is made. Arunachal accounts for a varied datable chronology deciphered so far spanning over from Palaeolithic Culture to fifteenth century A.D. which itself shows both Ancient and Medieval historical occurrences of Arunachal Pradesh within it. There is no definite and significant historical phenomenon occurring in the region which could be taken as a yardstick to differentiate medieval from that of ancient as is the justification in case of periodisation of Ancient and Medieval Indian history. If Ancient Indian history begins with the Harappan culture from 2500 B.C. and ends up with 1000 A.D or 1200 A.D. and the Medieval Indian history with the advent of the Muslims as the dominating political power, no such evidences are available so far in Arunachal Pradesh in order to ascertain their contemporaneity with Indian.

If we take Assam as a feeder region with which Arunachal Pradesh had some accessibility, a different kind of historical mooring emerges in a medieval set up. Here, in case of Assam the advent of Muslims does not play as significant a role as the advent of Ahoms, in testifying its corroboration to the criterion for periodisation of medieval Indian history. If it is so with Assam it was far less with Arunachal Pradesh, practically showing nil influence of the Muslims on its history and politics.

The above discussion shows a complete different historical development in Arunachal Pradesh in comparison to the history of Northern India. If we take dynastic history as parameter it is difficult to periodise the history of Arunachal Pradesh in the above chronological framework. The political and dynastic history is completely missing from the annals of Arunachal history right from the ancient period to the modern with the absence of kingdom and their rule except those of the genealogical and migrational myths of the tribes and tribal politics. It is difficult to trace out the relations of the Arunachal tribes with the outside world prior to the sixteenth century A.D. due to want of any authentic record.

Hence politically and culturally Arunachal Pradesh was still in her ancient character upto the early years of India's independence when North India being transformed from her Ancient to Medieval and from Medieval to Modern. It is relevant to ask, can we fix 1523 A.D. (if first ever Ahom-Arunachal relations in the form of Adi-Ahom relations are taken justifiably), as the terminal date for the end of Ancient period and beginning of the Medieval period in the history of Arunachal Pradesh? Similarly it is difficult to characterise the period from 1523 A.D. to the British relation with Arunachal Pradesh in 1825 (if the

British nexus with the tribes which began as early as 1825 is taken as the criterion for the end of medieval period and beginning of the modern period) as the Medieval period. No doubt, the Ahom-tribal relations brought some socio-economic and political changes in the then Arunachal, but significant changes were absent on the basis of which the historians cannot construct vital pillars of medieval history.

The British also developed their relations with Arunachal Pradesh in different phases. In the Western side, while they started developing relations with the Akas as early as 1825, with the Shertukpens as early as 1836 and the Bhutias as early as 1838; in the Central region, their relations began with the Adis as early as 1825, with the Nyishis as early as 1835 and with the Apatanis as early as 1895 and in the Eastern side, they had their relations with Mishmis and Singphos as early as 1825 and with the Khamptis as early as 1830. So it is difficult to fix any terminal date for the beginning of the modern period in Arunachal history.

The above evidences prove beyond the doubt the fact that the periodisation of Indian history into the said chronological framework of Ancient, Medieval and Modern cannot be strictly applied to periodise the history of Arunachal Pradesh. It is still a perplexed chapter of the history of the state on which serious attention has to be delved into. Which are the facts to be put under the framework of Ancient, Medieval and Modern history of Arunachal; from where to where this periodisation is to stick to; what should be the accepted terminal date to fix the beginning and end of such periodisation and what should be the criterion for such periodisation; are some of the important queries which haunt the scholars having interests in the history of Arunachal Pradesh. Absence of Carbon- 14 evidences has posed great challenges before the historians to substantiate the validity of periodisation. A fateful periodisation based upon logical framework is expected to bring out scholastic enthusiasm and determination among the researchers in the region.

Given the type of discussion held above the history of Arunachal Pradesh can justifiably be periodised into four sections, i.e., Pre-history, Proto-history, Pre-British and British. While the archaeological remains from Palaeolithic to Neolithic can be classified as Pre-history, the sculptural remains dealing with religious icons, inscriptions, epigraphic documents and oral sources can certainly be ascribed to Proto-history. Similarly the period from1523 to 1826 (1523 A.D. being the initial year of the Ahom-Arunachal relations in the form of Adi-Ahom relations; and 1826 A.D. being the year of conquest of Assam by the British after the Treaty of Yandaboo) can be put as the Pre-British period. The British relations with the tribes of the state in the post-1826 times till India got independence can also safely be termed as the British period of the history of Arunachal Pradesh.

References

1. V.C.P. Choudhury, *Secularism vs. Communalism*, Patna, 1977.
2. A.K. Thakur, *India and the Afghans*, Patna, 1992, pp.195-96.
3. O.P. Kejariwal, "The Indian History Congress and Historical Research in North-East India", *Proceedings of NEIHA*, 8th Session, Kohima, 1987, p.40.
4. H.L. Gupta, "Presidential Address", *Proceedings of NEIHA*, Sixth Session, Agartala, 1985, pp.19-20.
5. Satish Saberwal, "Oral Data, Religious Literature and History-Notes from a Sociologist", in *History and Society*, edited by D. Chattopadhyay, Calcutta, 1976.

Bibliography

Primary Sources

Report of Maxwell, Foreign Department, Ext. A, Progg., October 18, 1914, Nos.41-116.

Selection of Papers; Regarding the Hill Tracts between Assam and Burma and on the Upper Brahmaputra, 1825-70, Calcutta, 1873.

See *North and North-East Frontier Tribes of India*, compiled in Intelligence Branch Division of the Chief of the British Army Staff, New Delhi, 1945.

Secondary Sources

Ahmed, Leila, *Women and Gender in Islam*, New Haven and London: Yale University Press, 1992.

Aitchison, C. U., *A Collection of Treaties, Engagements and Sanads,* Vol. XII, 1973 (Reprint), Government of India Central Publication Branch.

Al-Azmeh, Aziz, 'Muslim History: Reflections on Periodisation and Categorisation', *The Medieval History Journal*, Vol. 1, No. 2, (1998).

Allchin, Bridget and Raymond, *The Rise of Civilization in India and Pakistan*, New Delhi 1983.

Allen, B. C., *Assam District Gazetteer*: Nagaland and Manipur, Shillong, 1905.

Ashraf, A. A., *Pre-historic Archaeology of Lower Subansiri District of Arunachal Pradesh,* Department of Research, Government of Arunachal Pradesh, Itanagar, 1990.

Ashraf, A. A., *Pre-historic Arunachal*: *A Study of Pre-historic and Ethnoarchaeology of Kamla Valley*, Department of

Research, Government of Arunachal Pradesh, Itanagar, 1990.

Badauni, Mulla Abdul Qadir, *Muntakhab al-Tawarikh*, (ed.), Maulvi Ahmad Ali, Calcutta, 1869.

Barkataki, S., *Tribes of Assam*, Shillong, 1968.

Barpujari, H. K., *Problem of Hill Tribes: North East Frontier (1822-42*), Vol. I, Gauhati, 1970.

Barpujari, H. K., *Problem of Hill Tribes: North East Frontier (1843-72),* Vol. II, Gauhati, 1976.

Barua, G., Ahom Buranji, Gauhati, 1930.

Barua, K. L., *Early History of Kamarupa*, Gauhati, 1966.

Baruah, S. L., *A Comprehensive History of Assam*, New Delhi, 1977.

Beams, J., *Outline of Indian Philology*, Calcutta, 1867, Appendix.

Beresford, C. W., *Notes on the North East Frontier of Assam*, Shillong, 1881.

Bezbaruah, R., *North East India: Interpreting the Sources of its History*, Delhi, 2007.

Biswas, N. B., 'Historical Research in Arunachal Pradesh: Oral Source and Method', *PNEIHA*, Thirteenth Session, Shillong, 1992.

Bloch, Marc, *The Historian's Craft*, Manchester University Press, Manchester, 1954.

Bora, D. K., Ashraf A.A. and Dutta, J.C., *Medieval Life at Naksaparvat*, Department of Research, Government of Arunachal Pradesh, Itanagar, 1990.

Bose, M. L., *British Policy in the North East Frontier Agency*, New Delhi, 1979.

Bose, M. L., *Emergence of Arunachal Pradesh: A Study in Administrative Growth*, New Delhi, 1978.

Bose, M. L., *History of Arunachal Pradesh*, New Delhi, 1997.

Butler, John, 'Rough Notes on Angami Nagas', *Journal of Asiatic Society of Bengal*, Vol. 44, No. 4, 1875.

Callinicos, Alex, *Theories and Narratives: Reflections on the Philosophy of History*, Polity Press, Cambridge, 1995.

Campbell, G., *Specimens of the Languages of India including those of the Aboriginal Tribes of Bengal, the Central Provinces and the Eastern Frontier*, Calcutta, 1874.

Carr, E. H., *What is History*, London, 1961.

Chakravarty, L. N., *Glimpses of the Early History of Arunachal*, Directorate of Research, Government of Arunachal Pradesh, Itanagar, 1995.

Chatterjee, Subid, *A Comprehensive History of Arunachal Pradesh,* Calcutta, 1991.

Chatterjee, S. K., 'Kirata- Jana Krit, Indo- Mongoloids: Their Contribution to the History and Culture of India', *Journal of Royal Asiatic Society of Bengal,* Vol. XVI, No. 2, Calcutta, 1950.

Chatterjee, S. K., "Kirata- Jana Krit", *Journal of Royal Asiatic Society of Bengal,* Vol. XVI, Calcutta, 1950.

Chatterjee, Subas, *Mizoram under British Rule*, Delhi, 1985.

Chattopadhyaya, B. D., 'State and Economy in North India: 4th century to twelfth century' in Romila Thapar (ed.), *Recent Perspectives of Early Indian History,* Bombay, 1995.

Chattopadhyaya, B. D., *The Making of Early Medieval India,* New Delhi, 1994.

Choudhury, V.C.P., *Secularism vs. Communalism*, Patna, 1977.

Chowdhury, J. N., *Arunachal Panorama*, Shillong, 1973.

Chowdhury, J. N., *Arunachal Through the Ages,* Shillong, 1982.

Collingwood, R. G., *The Idea of History*, OUP, 1988.

Cunning, R.C. R., 'Notes on Certain Frontier Tribes', *Census of India, 1921*, Shillong, 1923, Vol. III, Assam, Pt. 1, Report, App. B.

Dalton, E.T., *Descriptive Ethnology of Bengal*, Calcutta, 1872; German Edition: Berlin, 1875.

Das, Gurudas, 'Incorporation of Arunachal Hills into Colonial British India: A Politico- Economic Analysis', *PNEIHA*, Doimukh, 1994.

De, Barun, 'Encapsulation as an Alternative to the Difficulties of Periodising Indian History', in S.C. Malik Ed. *Indian*

Civilisation, The First Phase Problem of a Source Book, IIAS, Simla 1971.

Devi, Laxmi, *Ahom-Tribal Relations*, Calcutta, 1968 (2nd Edn. 1992).

Dubey, S. M., *Modernisation and Elites in Arunachal Pradesh,* Census of India, Delhi, 1971.

Dunbar, G., *Other Men's Lives*, London, 1938.

Dutta, S. (ed), *Studies* in the *History, Economy* and *Culture* of *Arunachal Pradesh,* Itanagar, 2000.

Elton, G., *The Practice of History*, Fontana, London, 1969.

Elwin, V., *India's North East Frontier in the Nineteenth Century*, Oxford University Press, 1962.

Elwin, V., *North East India in nineteenth Century*, Shillong, 1959.

Engels, *Origin of Family, Private Property and the State*, Moscow, 1950.

Fritz, John M, Michell, George and Devraj, D.V., Vijayanagara, Research Project monographs (5 Vols. on various themes), New Delhi, various dates around 1995.

Furer-Haimendorf, C. V., *Highlanders of Arunachal Pradesh*, New Delhi, 1982.

Gait, E., *A History of Assam*, Reprint, Calcutta, 1967.

Gait, Edward, *History of Assam*, Calcutta, 1905, Reprint 1984.

Geyl, P., *Debates with Historians*, Fontana, London, 1962.

Goswami Priyam, *The History of Assam- From Yandabo to Partition, 1824-1947*, Orient Blackswan, New Delhi, 2012.

Goswami, S. D., 'Progress of Historical Research in North East India: A Survey', (*PNEIHA*), 14th Session, Jorhat, 1993.

Green, William A., 'Periodisation in European and World History', *Journal of World History*, Vol. III, No. 1, 1992.

Grewal, J. S., *Medieval India: History and Historians*, Amritsar, 1975.

Guha, Amalendu, 'Presidential Address', North East India History Association, Dibrugarh, 1981.

Gupta, H.L., "Presidential Address", *Medieval section of Indian History Congrees Banaras session, 1969.*

Habib, Irfan, 'Presidential Address', Medieval Section of the *Indian History Congress*, Banaras Session, 1969.

Habib, Irfan, *People's History of India* (three volumes) New Delhi, 2001, 2002 & 2003.

Hamilton, A., *In Abor Jungles of North East India*, Delhi, 1984 (Reprint).

Hannay, S. F., *Sketch of the Singphos or the Kakhyens of Burma*, Calcutta, 1847, Tract 266.

Hore, Capt. W. B., *Report on the Abor Country*, Simla, 1913.

Jenkins, Keith, *Re-thinking History*, Routledge, 1991.

Jha, B. N., 'Politics of Posa: A Case Study of Pre and Post Independence Scenario in Arunachal Pradesh and Assam', *Proceedings of the Indian History Congress*, 57th Session, Madras University, 1996.

Jha, D. N., *Feudal Social Formation in Early India*, Delhi, 1987.

Jha, S. D., *Arunachal Pradesh- Rich Land Poor People*, New Delhi, 1986.

Kejariwal, O. P., 'The North-East in Indian Historiography: The Need for a Corrective', *PNEIHA*, Pasighat, 1986.

Kejariwal, O.P., "The Indian History Congress and Historical Research in North-East India", *Proceedings of NEIHA*, 8th Session, Kohima, 1987.

Khalidi, Tarif, 'Reflections on Periodisation in Arabic Historiography', *The Medieval History Journal*, Vol. 1, No. 1, (1998).

Kosambi, D. D., '*On a Marxist Approach to Indian Chronology*' in Combined Methods in Indology and Other Writings (Ed. B. Chattopadhyaya), New Delhi, 2002, (originally published in 1951).

Kosambi, D. D., *An Introduction to the Study of Indian History*, Bombay, 1956.

Kosambi, D. D., *The Culture and Civilisation of Ancient India in Historical Outline*, New Delhi 1981.

Kulke, Hermann (ed.), *State in India 1000-1700*, Delhi, 1995.

Lal, Kishori Saran, *History of the Khaljis A.D. 1290-1320*, Karachi, not dated.

Lamb, Alastair, *Britain and Chinese Central Asia*, London, 1960.

Lane-Poole, Stanley, *Medieval India Under Muhammedan Rule (A.D. 712-1764)*, Lahore, 1997, (first published 1903).

Leary, Brendan O', *The Asiatic Mode of Production: Oriental Despotism, Historical Materialism and Indian History*, Oxford and Cambridge, (Mass.), 1989.

Lego, N., *Ancient and Medieval History of Arunachal Pradesh (From the Earliest Times to1824)*, Itanagar, 2006.

Lego, N., *Modern History of Arunachal Pradesh (1825-2006)*, Itanagar, 2006.

Lepper, C. H., 'Notes on the Singpho and Khampti Country of North East Frontier', *Proceedings of Asiatic Society of Bengal*, Calcutta, 1882.

Mackenzie, A., *History of the Relations of the Government with the Hill Tribes of the North-East Frontier of Bengal*, Calcutta, 1884.

Majumdar, R. C. (et al.), *An Advanced History of India*, London, 1950.

Malik, S. C. (Ed.), *Indian Civilisation, The First Phase Problem of a Source Book*, IIAS, Simla 1971.

Marx, Karl, *A Contribution to the Critique of Political Economy*, Moscow, 1970.

Mibang, Tamo,' Origin and Migration of the Tribals of Tirap', *PNEIHA,* Twelfth Session, Jagiroad, 1991.

Mill, James, *The History of British India*, New York, 1968.

Morony, M., *Iraq after the Muslim Conquest*, Princeton, 1984.

Mukherjee, B. N., 'On Periodisation' in S.C. Malik Ed. *Indian Civilisation, The First Phase Problem of a Source Book*, IIAS, Simla 1971.

Mukhia, Harbans, 'Medieval India: An Alien Conceptual Hegemony?', *The Medieval History Journal*, Vol. 1, No. 1, (1998).

Mukhia, Harbans, 'Was there Feudalism in India?', *The Journal of Peasant Studies*, Vol. 8, No. 3., April 1981.

Munslow, Alun, *Deconstructing History*, Routledge, 1997.

Nag, Sajal, 'Aspects of Historiography of North East India', *PNEIHA*, Aizawl, 1996.

Nair, P. T., *Tribes of Arunachal Pradesh*, Guwahati, 1985.

Needham J. F., *Outline Grammar of the Khampti Language*, Shillong, 1894.

Needham J. F., *Report of a Trip into the Abor Hills, 1884,* Shillong, 1895.

Needham, J. F., *Outline Grammar of the Singpho Language*, Shillong, 1889.

Nizami, K. A. (ed.), *Politics and Society during the Early Medieval Period: Collected Works of Professor Mohammad Habib,* Delhi, 1974.

Novak, George, *Understanding History*, Pathfinder Press, New York, 1972.

Osik, N. N. *Modern History of Arunachal Pradesh*, Itanagar/ Delhi, 1999.

Osik, N. N., *A Brief History of Arunachal Pradesh*, New Delhi, 1996.

Palit, D. K., *Sentinels of the North East: The Assam Rifles*, New Delhi, 1984.

Pandey, B. B., *Arunachal Pradesh From Village to Statehood*, Itanagar, 1997.

Pandey, D. and Tripathy, B. K., *A Comprehensive History of Arunachal Pradesh*, Pasighat, 1997.

Pemberton, R. B., *Report on the Eastern Frontier of the British India,* Calcutta, 1835.

Phukan, K. T., *Assam Buranji: A Chronicle of the Ahom Rule in Assam (1228-1826)*, Sibsagar, 1848.

Proceedings of the Indian History Congress, 13th Session, Nagpur, 1950 and 14th Session, Jaipur, 1951.

Raiker, Y. A. & Chatterji, S., *Archaeology in Arunachal Pradesh*, Shillong, 1980.

Raiker, Y. A., *Ita Fort*, Shillong, 1978.

Ray, Himanshu Prabha & Sinopoli, Carlo M. (Ed), *Archaeology as History in Early South Asia*, Aryan Books International, Delhi, 2004.

Ray, N. R., 'The Medieval Factor in Indian History, General President's Address', *Proceedings of the Indian History Congress*, 29th Session, Patiala, 1967.

Reid, R., *History of the Frontier Areas Bordering Assam, 1883-1941*, New Delhi, 1983.

Reuter, Timothy, 'Medieval: Another Tyrannous Construct?', *The Medieval History Journal*, Vol. 1, No. 1, (1998).

Robinson, W., 'Notes on the Daphlas and the Peculiarities of their Language', *Journal of the Asiatic Society of Bengal* (*JASB*), No. 2, 1851.

Robinson, W., *A Descriptive Account of Assam*, Reprint, New Delhi, 1975.

Saberwal, Satish, "Oral Data, Religious Literature and History-Notes from a Sociologist", in *History and Society*, edited by D. Chattopadhyay, Calcutta, 1976.

Sangma, M. S., 'Presidential Address', *PNEIHA*, 15th Session, Doimukh, 1994.

Sarkar, J., *Society, Culture and Ecological Adaptation among Three Tribes of Arunachal Pradesh*, Calcutta, 1987.

Settar, S & Korisetta r(Ed), *Indian Archaeology in Retrospect, Proto-History: Archaeology of the Harappan Civilization*, Vol. II, Manohar Publishers, Delhi, 2002.

Settar, S & Korisettar (Ed*), Indian Archaeology in Retrospect, Archaeology and Interactive Disciplines*, Vol. III, Manohar Publishers, Delhi, 2002.

Settar, S & Korisettar (Ed), *Indian Archaeology in Retrospect, Archaeology and Historiography, History, Theory and Method*, Vol. IV, Manohar Publishers, Delhi, 2002.

Settar, S & Korisettar (Ed), *Indian Archaeology in Retrospect, Pre-History: Archaeology of South Asia*, Vol. I, Manohar Publishers, Delhi, 2002.

Shakespeare, L. W., *History of Upper Assam, Upper Burma and North-East Frontier*, London, 1914.

Sharma, R. S., 'Problem of Transition from Ancient to Medieval in Indian History', *The Indian Historical Review*, Vol. I, No.1, 1974.

Singh, Chandrika, *Emergence of Arunachal Pradesh as a State*, Delhi, 1989.

Singh, Chandrika, *Political Evolution of Nagaland*, New Delhi, 1981.

Singh, J. P. and Sengupta, G., *Archaeology of North Eastern India*, New Delhi, 1991.

Singh, K. S. (Ed), *People of India- Arunachal Pradesh*, Vol.XIV, Calcutta, 1995.

Singh, K. S. (ed), *Problem of Hill Tribes: North East Frontier (1873-1962)*, Vol. III, Gauhati, 1981.

Smith, W. C., 'Missionary Activities and the Acculturation of Backward People', *Journal of Applied Sociology,* Vol. 7, Calcutta, 1923.

Smith, W. C., *The Naga Tribes of Assam*, London, 1825.

Stalin, Joseph, *Dialectical and Historical Materialism*, *History of the CPSU (B) Short Course,* Moscow, 1951.

Subbarao, B., *The Personality of India*, Baroda, 1958.

Suleykin, D. A., *Basic Questions of the Periodisation of Ancient Indian History*, Calcutta, 1954.

Syiemlieh, D. R., *British Administration in Meghalaya: Policy and Pattern*, New Delhi, 1989.

Talukdar, A. C., 'Political Evolution of Arunachal Pradesh', *Proceedings of North East India History Association* (hence PNEIHA), Pasighat, 1986.

Tambs-Lyche, Harald, *Power, Profit and Poetry. Traditional Society in Kathiawar, Western India,* New Delhi, 1997.

Thakur, A. K., Archaeology of Arunachal Pradesh, *ICHR Project Report*, New Delhi, 2004.

Thakur, A.K., *India and the Afghans*, Patna, 1992.

Thapar, R., Mukhia, H. & Chandra, Bipan, Communalism and Writings of Indian History, People's Publishing House, 2nd Edition, New Delhi, 1977.

Thapar, R., *The Past and Prejudice,* Sardar Patel Memorial Lecture, New Delhi, 1975.

Thapar, Romila (ed.), *Recent Perspectives of Early Indian History,* Bombay, 1995.

Thapar, Romila, *'Towards the Definition of an Empire: The Mauryan State'* in Romila Thapar, Cultural Pasts, New Delhi, 2000 (originally published in 1987).

Tosh, J., *The Pursuit of History,* Longman, London, 1984.

White, Hayden, 'The Politics of Historical Interpretation: Discipline and De- sublimation', *The Content of the Form: Narrative Discourse and Historical Representation,* Johns Hopkins University, Baltimore and London, 1987.

White, J. C., *Sikkim and Bhutan,* Delhi, 1971.

Wink, Andre', *Al-Hind: The Making of the Indo-Islamic World,* Volume I: Early Medieval India and the Expansion of Islam, 7th –11th Centuries, New Delhi, 1999.

Woodthorpe, R. G, 'Notes on the Wild Tribes inhabiting the so-called Naga Hills on North- East Frontier of India', *Journal of Royal Anthropological Institute,* Vol. II, Calcutta, 1882.

Yonuo, Asoso, *The Rising Nagas: A Historical and Political Study,* Delhi, 1974.

Index